TEACHER
EVALUATION
AND
STUDENT
ACHIEVEMENT

The Authors

James H. Stronge is Heritage Professor in the Educational Policy, Planning, and Leadership Area at the College of William and Mary in Williamsburg, Virginia. One of his primary research interests is in educational personnel evaluation. He has worked with numerous educational organizations to design and develop evaluation systems for teachers and support personnel. He is the author or co-author of numerous articles, books, and technical reports on teacher, administrator, and support personnel evaluation. His authored or edited publications include the books *Evaluating Professional Support Personnel in Education* (Sage Publications), *Evaluation Handbook for Professional Support Personnel* (Center for Research on Educational Accountability and Teacher Evaluation), and *Evaluating Teaching: A Guide to Current Thinking and Best Practice* (Corwin Press). Stronge served as director of the Evaluating Professional Support Personnel project conducted by the Center for Research on Educational Accountability and Teacher Evaluation (CREATE). Currently, he is associate editor of the *Journal of Personnel Evaluation in Education*. He received his doctorate in educational administration and planning from the University of Alabama. He has been a teacher, counselor, and district-level administrator.

Pamela D. Tucker is an assistant professor of education at the University of Virginia and Director of the Principal Internship Program in the Curry School of Education. She earned her doctorate in educational administration from the College of William and Mary. Her research focuses on various aspects of personnel evaluation, including legal and ethical considerations, and the development of aspiring principals. She is co-author of a book, *Evaluation Handbook for Professional Support Personnel* (Center for Research on Educational Accountability and Teacher Evaluation), and several articles, including "Legal Context for Teacher Evaluation," "The Principal's Role in Evaluating Professional Support Personnel," and "Evaluating School Counselors." Other activities in the area of personnel evaluation include membership on the editorial review board of the *Journal of Personnel Evaluation in Education*. She served as co-editor with James H. Stronge of a special issue on the politics of personnel evaluation. As a special education teacher and former administrator in a school for learning disabled students, she has worked with a variety of student populations and has a particular concern for those most at risk of school failure. As an outgrowth of her experience as Program Administrator for the Virginia homeless education grant, she has recently published "Enhancing Collaboration on Behalf of Homeless Students: A Multi-faceted Response to a Complex Problem" in the *Journal for a Just and Caring Society.*

Student Assessment Series

TEACHER EVALUATION AND STUDENT ACHIEVEMENT

James H. Stronge and Pamela D. Tucker

Glen W. Cutlip
Series Editor

NATIONAL EDUCATION ASSOCIATION

Note

The opinions expressed in this publication should not be construed as representing the policy or position of the National Education Association. These materials are intended to be discussion documents for educators who are concerned with specialized interests of the profession.

Reproduction of any part of this book must include the usual credit line and copyright notice. Address communications to Editor, NEA Teaching and Learning.

Library of Congress Cataloguing-in-Publication Data

Stronge, James H.
    Teacher evaluation and student achievement/ James H. Stronge and Pamela D. Tucker.
      p. cm.—(Student assessment series)
    Includes bibliographical references.
    ISBN 0-8106-2073-1
    1. Teachers—Rating of—United States. 2. Teacher effectiveness—United States 3. Academic achievement—United States. I. Tucker, Pamela D. II. Title. III. Series.
    LB2838.S82 2000
    371.14'4—dc21   02-020056
                                                  CIP

CONTENTS

INTRODUCTION

The field of student assessment—from methodology and techniques to the use of results—is changing, and the changes are dramatically affecting the work of education employees. Student assessment is a major part of every teacher's work, and increasingly, student achievement is used as a measure of teacher performance.

Changes in student assessment have created new concerns for teachers, especially in the use of assessment results. Today, those results are being used for more than comparing an individual student's performance against a state or national norm, and for more than providing data for making program improvement decisions. They are being used to determine the success or failure of teachers and schools. Policy makers and others are using large-scale assessments to decide whether teachers and schools are providing an adequate education to all students and attaching consequences, positive and negative, on the basis of student assessment results. The use of student test scores has raised the stakes for all education employees.

Nearly one-third of a classroom teacher's time is spent assessing and evaluating student performance. Indeed, many influential groups have identified competence in student assessment as essential for the training and licensing of new teachers and the upgrading of the skills of practicing teachers (National Board for Professional Teaching Standards, Interstate New Teacher Assessment Consortium, National Council for Accreditation of Teacher Education, Educational Testing Service, and the National Association of State Directors of Teacher Education and Certification). These groups estimate that less than one-half of currently practicing teachers have received adequate training in student assessment, and yet their performance may be judged on their ability to match their students' performance to assessment criteria.

To help members and other educators keep abreast of the ever-changing field of student assessment and teacher evaluation, the National Education Association (NEA) has commissioned leading assessment and evaluation experts to write about these related issues from their own perspectives. Experts James H. Stronge and Pamela D. Tucker, the authors of this book on teacher evaluation and student achievement, believe that the results of student assessments are becoming ever more important in the lives of teachers through the use of student achievement as an evaluative criterion for their work. In this book, they discuss four distinct approaches to incorporating student achievement in teacher evaluation. Each approach is described with its advantages and disadvantages identified. The book is intended to be of use to teachers at all levels, preschool through graduate studies, as well as to other education employees.

The NEA has developed the Student Assessment Series to help teachers and other education employees improve their knowledge and skills in student assessment and achievement and hopes readers will find the series a valuable resource for current and future student assessment and teacher evaluation practices.

Glen W. Cutlip
Series Editor

I.

TEACHER EVALUATION AND STUDENT ACHIEVEMENT: AN INTRODUCTION TO THE ISSUES

What is the most significant school influence on student achievement? Systemic school reform programs? Curriculum alignment? Higher standards? Lower class size? Early childhood programs? Parental involvement? To varying degrees, there is evidence that these and other strategies can be catalysts to improve schools and increase student learning.[1] But what is the single most influential factor on student achievement? It is the teacher.

What Is the Evidence That Teachers Matter?

Virtually all of us can recite the names of teachers who have played significant roles in our learning and lives—sometimes significant even to the point of career changing. One researcher who examined the autobiographies of 125 prominent Americans from the nineteenth and twentieth centuries found that they consistently described good teachers in their lives as having "competence in the subject matter, caring deeply about students and their success, and character, distinctive character."[2] Clearly, there are distinctive qualities that epitomize good teachers—and one of those qualities is the ability to make a difference in students' lives. Anyone who has ever had an outstanding teacher knows emphatically that yes, teachers do make a difference. What we have known intuitively all along now can be answered empirically: teachers absolutely, unequivocally, make a difference in student learning. To support this claim, we offer a brief glimpse of three different studies that have come to the same conclusion: *teachers matter.*

Certified Versus Non-certified Teachers

One statewide study conducted at the University of Texas at Arlington found that students taught by teachers certified in the subjects they teach outperformed students taught by out-of-field teachers on the Texas state student assessment system. Based on 1996-97 data for most of the state's teachers, the researchers found that 75.3 percent of third graders passed the Texas Assessment of Academic Skills (TAAS) when taught by teachers in their certification field, as compared with 63.7 percent passing when fewer than 85 percent of the students' teachers were certified. The findings were similar for Hispanic and Black students, with both groups experiencing higher pass rates when their teachers were certified in their teaching fields.[3] As the president of one of Texas' professional teacher associations stated, "Imagine how well all our students would do if all students had qualified teachers."[4]

Teachers' Additive Effect on Student Learning

The work of Bill Sanders at the University of Tennessee's Value-Added Research and Assessment Center over the past several years has been groundbreaking in terms of expanding our understanding of the relationship between teacher quality and student learning.[5] Findings on the additive effect of teachers on student achievement have been one important aspect of the work of Sanders and his colleagues.

Over a multi-year period, Sanders has focused on what happens to students who have teachers who produce high student achievement compared with students placed with teachers whose classes produce low achievement results. He discovered that when children, beginning in third grade, were placed with three high performing teachers in a row, they scored, on average, at the 96th percentile on Tennessee's statewide mathematics assessment at the end of fifth grade. When children with comparable achievement histories starting in third grade were placed with three low performing teachers in a row, their average score on the same mathematics assessment was at the 44th percentile.[6] By comparison, that is an enormous 52-percentile point difference!

Elaborating on this body of research, Sanders and colleagues reported the following:

> the results of this study well document that the most important factor affecting student learning is the teacher. In addition, the results show wide variation in effectiveness among teachers. The immediate and clear implication of this finding is that seemingly more can be done to improve education by improving the effectiveness of teachers than by any other single factor. Effective teachers appear to be effective with students of all achievement levels, regardless of the level of heterogeneity in their classrooms.[7]

They added that "this finding is corroborated by recent research on the cumulative effects of teachers on the academic progress of students.[8]...These recent studies show that teacher effects on student learning as inferred from standardized test scores are additive and cumulative over grade levels with little evidence of compensatory effects."[9] Given results like these, it is no wonder that the researchers found that "a major conclusion is that teachers make a difference."[10]

Teachers' Residual Effect on Student Learning

Summarizing research from the Dallas Public Schools' Accountability System, Bob Mendro described the common misconception that "if teacher A doesn't do a good job this year, teacher B will make up for it next year. The Dallas data strongly suggest that negative effects of a teacher in the bottom third of effectiveness last through three years of teachers in the top third of effectiveness."[11] The good news is that if a child has a high performing teacher one year, she will enjoy the advantage of that good teaching in future years. Unfortunately, the converse also is true: if a child has a low performing teacher, she simply will not outgrow the negative effects of that year of lost learning opportunities for years to come. Furthermore, exacerbating the negative effects of poor performing teachers, the Dallas research shows that "lower-achieving students are more likely to be put with lower effectiveness teachers...Thus, the negative effects of less effective teachers are being visited on students who probably need the most help."[12]

Summarizing studies from both Dallas and the Tennessee Value-Added Assessment System, Mendro stated:

> Research...[13] has demonstrated the effects of teachers on student achievement. They [the researchers] show that there are large additional components in the longitudinal effects of teachers, that these effects are much larger than expected, and that the least effective teachers have a long-term influence on student achievement that is not fully remediated for up to three years later.[14]

In straightforward terms, what these residual effects studies make clear is that not only does teacher quality matter when it comes to how much students learn, but also that a teacher's effectiveness—for good or bad—stays with students for years to come.

What Is the Impetus for Using Student Achievement in Teacher Evaluation?

On a single day in 1999, *The Washington Post* carried paid advertisements from the National Education Association and the Mobil Corporation, as well as an editorial from nationally syndicated columnist David Broder—all with a common message: schools must be held accountable for results.

- In the NEA advertisement, "Show Me the Data!" President Bob Chase, in describing school reform, stated that "probably the best indicator of this new maturity is the intensive focus on education's bottom line: student achievement. It no longer suffices to come up with a new school reform program, couched in nothing more than high-sounding but vague rhetoric. Today educators, policy makers, and parents want to know whether or not a reform program will improve student learning."[15]

- The Mobil Corporation, in its advertisement, "Are schools improving? Too many educated guesses," described their concern, which is shared with the general business community: "As a company, we are only as good as our resources. We measure these not only in barrels of oil, refineries and laboratories but also in the skills of our employees...Because Mobil operates in so many diverse locales, we are all too familiar with the stubborn problems afflicting education in America: the lack of rigor and consistency in student and teacher standards, assessments and accountability."[16]
- David Broder, in his editorial, "No Magic for the Schools," discussed the challenges of enacting school accountability legislation being considered at that time by the California legislature. In the article, Broder quoted California Governor Gray Davis as saying, "We've had local control of schools for 50 years and it's been an abject failure. When you have an earthquake or natural disaster, people expect the state to intervene. Well, we have a disaster in our schools."[17]

The school accountability theme reflected in the three diverse interests described above is being repeated in states and local communities across America. Parents, policy makers, and educators alike, have examined the status of public schools and are calling for, even demanding, improvement. School reform efforts are taking a variety of forms, with one of the most prominent being a focus on higher teacher standards and improved student performance.

Given the central role that teachers have always played in successful schools, connecting teacher performance and student performance is a natural extension of the educational reform agenda. "The purpose of teaching is learning, and the purpose of schooling is to ensure that each new generation of students accumulates the knowledge and skills needed to meet the social, political, and economic demands of adulthood."[18] Thus, for many, it seems long overdue to assure that student learning gains are taken into account in the design and implementation of teacher evaluation systems.

Summary

The opening salvo in the 1996 report *What Matters Most: Teaching for America's Future* by the National Commission on Teaching and America's Future, is as follows:

> We propose an audacious goal. . .by the year 2006, America will provide all students in the country with what should be their educational birthright: access to competent, caring, and qualified teachers.[19]

The Commission followed this opening statement with its first of five major recommendations: *Get serious about standards for both students and teachers.* "Clearly, if students are to achieve high standards, we can expect no less from their teachers and other educators."[20]

If teachers do, in fact, make a difference in student learning, and if we are to have competent and caring teachers, shouldn't we relate teacher work to student work? Shouldn't student achievement be a fundamental measure of teacher effectiveness? We explore these questions in this edition of the NEA assessment series. This introductory chapter is followed by an overview of issues and research on the relationship between teaching and learning. Then, we examine, in turn, four examples of assessment systems that rely on student learning as a measure of teacher effectiveness:[21]

- Assessing Teacher Performance through Comparative Student Gain Scores: The Dallas Value-Added Accountability System
- Assessing Teacher Performance through Repeated Measures of Student Gains: The Tennessee Value-Added Assessment System
- Assessing Teacher Performance with Student Work: The Oregon Teacher Work Sample Methodology
- Assessing Teacher Performance in a Standards-based Environment: The Thompson, Colorado, School District.

In the concluding chapter we summarize key issues and offer recommendations for educators and policy makers who are interested in making the connection explicit between teacher evaluation and student achievement.

II.

WHAT IS THE RELATIONSHIP BETWEEN TEACHING AND LEARNING?

Is there a relationship between teaching and learning? What is the nature of that relationship? What is the responsibility of each party in facilitating the relationship? What other factors influence the relationship?

Elliot Eisner argues that as teachers "we are shapers of the environment, stimulators, motivators, guides, consultants, resources. But in the end, what children make of what we provide is a function of what they construe from what we offer."[22] While this is certainly true, educators have a greater influence on the learning that takes place than the argument suggests. Indeed, most educators view teaching and learning as a reciprocal process, an equal partnership, in which teachers and students alike shape the environment and support the learning endeavor through their thoughts and behaviors. There are clearly circumstances beyond the control of either students or teachers that interfere with the teaching and learning endeavor. Crowded, noisy cafeterias in which some classes must be held certainly impinge on education; hungry and sick children cannot learn despite the best efforts of teachers; and a lack of appropriate instructional materials can undermine any curriculum. However, assuming reasonable school and student conditions, most educators believe that teaching has not taken place if students have not learned.

Are Teachers Responsible for Student Learning?

As presented in chapter I, research strongly supports the contention that teachers and the quality of their instruction do affect student learning. Specific teacher behaviors such as those summarized by Brophy and Good[23] in the process-product research have positive effects on student achievement gains. Teachers can enhance learning gains through attention to the following areas:

1. appropriate expectations and a sense of efficacy
2. classroom management and organization
3. opportunity to learn
4. curriculum pacing
5. active teaching
6. teaching to mastery
7. supportive learning environment.[24]

Given the research base that exists on effective instructional practices, we believe that teachers can be responsible not only for good quality teaching, but also, to a reasonable extent, for positive learning outcomes. As noted by Brophy and Good, teacher effectiveness, in part, is considered to be a teacher's "success in fostering [students'] mastery of formal curricula."[25] If teachers can influence learning, then is it not a professional obligation to promote the greatest amount of learning possible?

Most teachers accept responsibility for student learning and are willing to be held accountable for results. As Roy Kemble, president of the Classroom Teachers of Dallas, an NEA affiliate, has observed, "every classroom teacher I've ever talked to, and I don't care what they're teaching, says they want to be accountable for what they do in their classrooms. They embrace it, they just want that accountability system to be fair."[26] Assuming this position is reflective of most teachers, then the question arises of how to measure learning outcomes and connect these measures to teacher evaluation in a fair manner.

How Can Student Learning Be Measured?

There is a long tradition of evaluating mastery of lessons learned, dating back to Plato. For centuries, students were assessed with oral exams, in most cases requiring them to recite specific passages or catechisms. In early America, the local school board often evaluated the teacher's effectiveness based on the recitation abilities of his or her students. Events such as spelling bees, for example, were public demonstrations of the skill of both students and their teachers. With the availability of paper and ever growing numbers of students in the nineteenth century, written exams began to take hold as a means of demonstrating a student's knowledge or eligibility for certain privileges.[27]

It was during the twentieth century that the modern standardized achievement test was developed. Thorndike, Terman, and others intended to create uniform scales in arithmetic, spelling, grammar, and other subjects to measure student learning such that it could be compared to the work of students anywhere in the country.[28] These uniform student assessment scales were intended to be more objective because they reflected a prescribed curriculum and eliminated the subjectivity or poor testing skill of the individual teacher. Today, standardized testing has become a political reality in the mandated programs that exist in almost every state.[29]

While tests are not sufficient to judge the whole of student learning or teacher effectiveness, they can provide information on various dimensions of learning, such as the acquisition of basic knowledge and skills. The information provided by tests seems to be a good starting point for identifying students who are having difficulty learning or teachers who are having difficulty teaching specific material. Sorting out where the problem lies and providing the needed assistance requires professional understanding of the dynamics of teaching and learning. Testing should not be used as a final judgment of failure or success, but as an indicator or source of information about possible problems that can be carefully unraveled by educators.

The critical role played by testing takes on particular urgency when it indicates the mastery of basic skills such as reading, writing, and computing. Without these skills, elementary students are truly doomed to failure, and we must identify these needs early and address them aggressively if we are to provide the foundation for all later learning. No amount of ingenious teaching can compensate for a student's lack of reading skills in the later grades. Poor reading skills compromise possible achievement throughout a student's school career. Tests are one means of ensuring a minimum standard of quality, especially for those children who are in the poorest schools, by illuminating the vast discrepancies in student achievement levels.

There is a range of possible strategies for assessing student learning, including standardized tests, informal inventories, performance assessments, and teacher-made tests. Standardized tests and performance assessments are being used most often for high-stakes assessment of learning. The standardized tests used most frequently in schools are "multiple-skill achievement tests that evaluate knowledge and understanding in several curricular areas."[30] They are group-administered and norm-referenced, providing comparisons with other students in the same grade across the country. In contrast, performance assessment is a "practice that requires students to create evidence through performance that will enable assessors to make valid judgments about 'what they know and can do' in situations that matter."[31] Eisner suggested the possibility that both standardized tests and performance assessments could be used with students to focus on both their general skills and particular talents. One would provide comparative data; the other, individualized reflections of student learning. Each assessment approach would complement the other by offering a different perspective of the student and acknowledging the competing demands of public education.

Should Student Learning Be Connected to Teacher Evaluation?

If teachers have a professional responsibility for enhancing learning, then it seems legitimate to explore the impact of the teacher's role in learning. The alternative is to evaluate only the process of teaching without regard to the effects on students; in essence, this would involve assessing the *means* of teaching and not the *ends*. For example, it has been common practice in school systems to judge teacher quality based on qualifications (college degree, licensure, and years of experience) and classroom observations. This input-process assessment approach is comparable to considering the merit of a given individual without regard to his or her value or ability to create value-added effect.

Traditional teacher evaluation practices that focus on process do not fully take into account the appropriateness of the instruction for a given audience. For example, a logical, well-paced, well-organized lesson plan does not guarantee learning for students if the teacher's vocabulary is too advanced for student understanding or if the foundation for the presented concepts has not been provided. While some observers may be able to ascertain signs of confusion and frustration for students, more direct measures of learning are important to clarify what has been understood and what has not. Strategies for measuring the process of teaching reveal only part of the exchange in teaching and learning, and they have limited scope.

The interaction between the teacher's efforts and the students' learning would seem to be the critical question in teacher evaluation. While clinical supervision has focused on teachers' instructional efforts with the intent of improving the teacher's expertise and enhancing student learning, a complementary strategy would be to measure the effects of instruction on students directly. Have students learned the knowledge and skills that reflect the conceptual framework for a given discipline? Can they build upon that foundation and embrace other areas of the discipline at a more advanced level?

Schalock and Schalock argued emphatically for this complementary strategy of assessing the effects of instruction, "looking at what teachers and schools accomplish, rather than what they do."[32] They elaborated further:

> We regard evidence of learning gains by students taught as the most important accomplishment to monitor. We argue that student learning is both the professional touchstone for teachers and the reason why schools exist, and that regardless of what else is examined in assessing a teacher's work or a school's worth, the learning gains of students taught must be taken into account.[33]

Teacher effectiveness has been found by researchers to have the greatest influence on student academic progress compared to an array of other possible factors, including previous achievement level, class size, poverty, and race.[34] Student progress (gains over the previous year), not student achievement level (based on national norms), reflects the true effects of schooling and is best predicted by teacher effectiveness. These findings confirm what most people have long believed: teacher quality is the most important factor in student learning. If this is the case, why not use measures of student learning for teacher evaluation? Is it not reasonable to expect teachers to meet the needs of most children in their classrooms most of the time, thereby yielding positive gains on measures of learning? Is it not reasonable to judge teaching by both its *means* (instructional processes) and its *ends* (instructional outcomes)?

How Can Student Learning Be Connected to Teacher Evaluation?

In the following chapters, we profile four accountability systems that link student assessment and teacher evaluation. Each system has unique features that were developed to enhance the fairness of using student learning measures as part of teacher evaluation. We will attempt to highlight the distinguishing features of these systems as well as the impact of their implementation.

III. ◆

ASSESSING TEACHER PERFORMANCE THROUGH COMPARATIVE STUDENT GROWTH: THE DALLAS VALUE-ADDED ACCOUNTABILITY SYSTEM

The Dallas Value-Added Accountability System is a locally designed and adapted response to the Texas state accountability system. It reflects years of conceptual and statistical work in the development of student predicted growth curves. For Dallas, the primary focus of accountability has been on growth, primarily the academic growth of students, but also the instructional growth of teachers and instructional leadership growth of principals. Previous student growth on a wide range of assessment measures is used to predict future growth of students. Effectiveness at the class and school level is determined by the *actual* progress achieved by students compared to the predicted or *expected* progress. The more actual student progress exceeds expected progress in the classroom, the greater the teacher's effectiveness or the "value-added" due to his or her instruction.[35] The more actual progress exceeds expected progress in the school, the greater the school staff's effectiveness. Based on the recommendation of the Dallas Commission for Educational Excellence, both monetary and recognition awards are now given to schools that exceed expected progress based on a number of measures, with money awarded to the school activity fund, professional personnel, and support personnel.[36]

What Are the Purposes of the Accountability System, and How Was It Developed?

Reflecting the situation in public schools across the country, Dallas' accountability system was developed "in response to demands for better schools and improved student performance."[37] With a unified perspective on what constitutes an effective school and classroom, outcome measures have been aligned to link the activities of school personnel in all instructional arenas. Webster and Mendro described the various purposes of the system in this way:

> The accountability system is multi-faceted, tying together district and campus improvement planning, principal and teacher evaluation, and school and teacher effectiveness. As such, all district elements directly related to student learning, from teaching in the classroom to campus instructional leadership to district curriculum and instruction and staff development programs are directly related to improvement on the same set of variables.[38]

Hence, the accountability system is closely connected to the teacher and principal appraisal systems.

Throughout the 1990s, the Dallas Independent School District (DISD) worked to refine its accountability practices to address concerns about fairness, arising from comparisons of students and schools with very different profiles around variables that impact achievement levels. The Accountability Task Force, a group with school and community representation, identified school level fairness variables (e.g., student mobility, overcrowding) and student background variables (e.g., limited English proficiency status, socioeconomic status) that are controlled in the statistical models to "level the playing field"[39] when comparisons are made across students and schools. There are additional safeguards built into the analyses that address common concerns of practitioners, such as student absences and longevity of enrollment.

What Are the Student Assessment Strategies?

The DISD uses an extensive array of standardized assessment measures in addition to the informal ones used in classrooms. The Texas Assessment of Academic Skills (TAAS) is mandated by the state and is supplemented by the Iowa Tests of Basic Skills (ITBS) in grades 1 through 8. For the upper grades (7-12), there are 150 end-of-course tests and a ninth grade achievement test in reading and mathematics. In addition, the DISD serves a large Hispanic population (49 percent), some of whom have limited English proficiency, and as such, there are two tests specifically targeted for Spanish speaking students. A detailed description of the assessment measures used to predict performance and the associated methodology is provided for DISD personnel in a document entitled *School Performance Improvement Awards*.[40] The following list summarizes the primary assessment instruments used by DISD:

- Iowa Tests of Basic Skills/Tests of Achievement and Proficiency—ITBS/TAP (Reading and Mathematics Total subtests in grades K-8)
- Texas Assessment of Academic Skills—TAAS (Reading and Mathematics in grades 3-8 and 10; Writing in grade 4; Writing, Social Studies, and Science in grade 8)

- Spanish Assessment of Basic Education—SABE (for LEP students in lieu of ITBS in grades 1-5)
- Woodcock-Munoz Language Survey—WMLS, Broad Ability Score (in grades K-11)
- Assessments of Course Performance—ACP (150 end of course criterion-referenced tests for core subjects in grades 7-12).

How Does the Accountability System Work?

As early as 1984, the DISD began "using multiple regression to develop longitudinal student growth curves on norm-referenced tests and to determine effectiveness by the degree to which schools exceeded their students' predicted growth."[41] This work provided the foundation for later efforts to measure school effectiveness and, more recently, classroom effectiveness. During this same time period, "statistical tools [became] available to control influences on multiple levels of variables and their associated bias,"[42] which had been a major challenge with previous efforts. In 1991, the Commission for Educational Excellence, appointed by the Dallas Board of Education, recommended an accountability system for schools and teachers based on student progress. Beginning in 1992, school effectiveness indices were generated, and in 1996, classroom effectiveness indices were formally adopted and introduced districtwide. In the meantime, during the 1995 session, the Texas Legislature mandated that teacher evaluation criteria be based, in part, on student performance. Thus, the classroom effectiveness indices were developed as a response to both local initiative and state mandate.

The Commission for Educational Excellence also emphasized the need for fairness in predicting student growth based on factors beyond the control of schools. Thus, the system uses a combination of multiple regression and hierarchical linear modeling to control for pre-existing student differences and school-level variables with the intent of creating a fair and equitable accountability system.

Reflective of the local commitment to broad-based participation in the development and refinement of accountability mechanisms, the Accountability Task Force was created and continues to review the system on a regular basis. The task force, which is "composed of parents, teachers, principals, and community and business representatives, serves as the final authority concerning variable selection and weighting, formulating the rules of the accountability system and the performance awards associated with it as well as hearing appeals of system decisions."[43] Also included in this group are representatives of the teacher organizations and a representative for an administrator organization. All stakeholders are part of the dialogue and decision-making process for determining the substance and procedures of the accountability system.

School Effectiveness Indices

School Effectiveness Indices were first developed in 1992. School effectiveness measures selected by the Accountability Task Force included a broad range of indices, with primary weighting given to test scores. The variety of criteria was greater at the high school level than at the lower levels, with the addition of variables such as percentage of students taking honors courses and graduation rates. Outcome measures used in 1997-98 were as follows:

- various tests noted above in assessment section (e.g., TAAS, ITBS, ACP)
- student attendance rates
- promotion rates
- dropout rates
- student enrollment in accelerated courses, honors courses, and advanced diploma plans
- graduation rates
- percentages of students taking college entrance exams.

Controlled school-level variables include "mobility, overcrowding, average family income, average family education level, poverty index, percentage minority, percentage of limited English proficient students, and percentage of students on free or reduced lunch."[44] These outcome variables are analyzed with a simple multiple regression model using two prior years of data for a school.

The Commission for Educational Excellence intended that the School Effectiveness Indices be used both to reward effective schools and to provide assistance and resources to ineffective schools.[45] Monetary awards are given to schools and their staffs when they meet the percent tested criteria (95 percent) and exceed growth predictions by one-half standard deviation. Awards include (a) an Outstanding School Improvement flag, (b) an Outstanding School Improvement plaque, (c) $2000 for the school activity fund, (d) $1000 for each professional personnel, and (e) $500 for each support personnel.[46]

School-based awards were supported over teacher-based awards with the explicit intent of encouraging cooperation and assistance. Research by Bearden, Bembry, and Babu[47] supported this approach. They found that a sense of community and teamwork distinguished effective schools from ineffective ones in the district. In schools identified as ineffective, a variety of strategies are used to improve student learning, including using available resources to train or retrain the staff, replacing administrators, or restructuring schools.[48]

Classroom Effectiveness Indices (CEIs)

Parallel to the School Effectiveness Indices, measures called Classroom Effectiveness Indices were developed to focus accountability efforts directly on student learning at the classroom level. The CEIs provide additional data to inform professional judgments, not supplant them. The indices were not intended for use as the sole criterion of effective teaching. DISD has encouraged the cautious use of CEIs and has provided training on the use and interpretation of the indices for principals and other administrators to enhance understanding. The indices "do not include, nor were they intended to include, formal diagnostic information about either the students or a teacher."[49] In the case of diagnostic information about teachers, this task is left to a process of assessment and assistance embedded in traditional supervision.

"To assure fairness, students are only compared with similar students based on ethnicity, gender, socioeconomic status, language proficiency, and previous levels of achievement."[50] "Student outcome variables are analyzed with a two-stage model. The first stage employs multiple regression to control the effects of the fairness variables; the second stage, a two-level hierarchical linear model (HLM), controls the effects of prior achievement or attendance and the influence of variables aggregated across the campus."[51]

Safeguards

There are numerous safeguards built into the Dallas accountability system that help protect against distortion of data. These include:

- School effectiveness is measured against performance of similar students across the entire school district. It is a contextually situated model that reflects curriculum, resources, students, and instructional personnel in the DISD.
- "The influence of important background variables of students, over which the schools have no control, are eliminated from the equations"[52] used to predict performance growth.
- Outcome variables are selected and weighted by the Accountability Task Force, which represents all constituencies.
- The continuous growth model applies to virtually all of the Dallas students. "Schools are required to test 95% of their continuously enrolled, non-exempt, regular, LEP, and special education students."[53] Exempt status is based on enrollment by the end of the first day of the second six weeks and necessary prior testing by DISD.[54]
- Only students who have been exposed to the DISD instructional program for most of the year are included in the classroom and school effectiveness measures. For example, students must have been enrolled continuously from the first day of the second six weeks and they must not have been absent more than 20 days to be used in calculations.
- When 11 students or fewer are used to calculate classroom effectiveness indices, caution is recommended in terms of interpretation.
- Comprehensive computerized cheating analyses are done on the classroom level test data to identify irregularities or unexpected changes in predicted growth curves.
- All educational staff receives training in the interpretation of test data.

How Is the Accountability System Related to Teacher Evaluation?

The teacher appraisal system is a diagnostic-prescriptive approach based on individualized instructional improvement plans with the explicit goal of "continually improving instruction using student outcomes."[55] The classroom effectiveness indices are used to identify needs and develop strategies to improve results. The process is analogous to principal evaluation, which is based on the school effectiveness indices and the development of campus improvement plans. The meshing of these parallel processes was intentional, designed to align efforts at the classroom, school, and district levels for more coordinated efforts in achieving the same goals.

The instructional improvement plan for teachers includes three sections: (a) needs, (b) concepts/content/strategies, and (c) documentation/evaluation. In collaboration with the appraiser, the teacher identifies needs based on instructional modifications suggested by assessment results of previous groups of students and predicted instructional targets based on testing of new students assigned to the teacher. Strategies are then keyed to student needs based on the assessment analysis of past and future students. The teacher and appraiser agree upon what constitutes evidence of successful strategy implementation and the timeline for data collection. For teachers with standardized test measures, these are used as one form of documentation. "Other data sources may include student profiles, portfolios, teacher-made tests, diagnostic skills analyses, and performance information."[56] For teachers without standardized test measures, alternative assessment measures, such as student performances, play a central role in documenting teacher accomplishments.

In addition to an analysis of mastered objectives on the various standardized tests as one means of identifying "needs," DISD has developed diagnostic tests called Diagnostic Skills Profiles that are administered twice a year. These diagnostic tests are not part of the accountability system but help to inform and focus classroom instructional efforts for core subject areas and give teachers an indication of mastery on the TAAS objectives.

It is important to note that teacher appraisal is based on the teacher's ability to meet student needs as identified in the instructional improvement plan. While the goal is to improve student learning, evaluation is focused on the teacher's efforts to improve instruction. Documentation of those efforts includes standardized test results for some teachers but is not limited to them, even in core subject areas. The classroom effectiveness indices are not intended to be a "final outcome measure of teacher effectiveness, [but a] starting point for identifying groups of teachers who are effective or ineffective relative to their students' measured achievement."[57] The instructional improvement plan is then used to focus teaching efforts to achieve better outcomes with students.

What Are the Advantages and Disadvantages of the Accountability System for Teacher Evaluation?

The Dallas Accountability System is a sophisticated approach to the quantification of student learning gains in a fair and bias-free manner. There are many advantages to it over the high stakes testing programs being used in other states, namely the fundamental focus on student gains versus absolute achievement levels. However, many disadvantages have also been identified and require further attention.

Advantages

- *The DISD accountability system focuses on continuous improvement and fairness.* A large majority of teachers (93 percent)[58] reported that the strategies that they identified in their Instructional Improvement Plans used in the teacher appraisal system were effective in increasing student learning during the 1997-98 school year.
- *With a focus on student improvement instead of achievement based on fixed standards, individual differences are identified and accommodated.* Students are expected to grow and improve but not necessarily at the same rate or to reach the same goal at the same time. Principals noted that by disaggregating and analyzing test data, they were able to target students who needed additional assistance and to refine instruction and professional development. Fall and spring diagnostic profiles also are used in conjunction with the formal testing to monitor student progress more carefully. The principals also used Student Support Teams to study the global needs of individual students and develop strategies to provide help. Possible educational strategies included tutoring, after-school programs, mentors from the community, summer school, and teacher adjusted instruction.
- *The DISD accountability system is a prime example of the technical advances in the analysis of student test score data.* A long-time observer of the DISD stated that it is important to note that this sophisticated system has evolved in a place where over the last "three decades, a remarkable assessment capacity has emerged...that capacity includes conceptualization, measurement, and dissemination competence."[59]
- *Classroom effectiveness indices provide a relatively simple measure of student progress and a teacher's ability to influence student learning outcomes.* Teachers, in general, did not object to the use of test data as an indicator of teaching effectiveness but felt strongly that it should not be used for a final judgment on effectiveness. They thought the test data should be considered over multiple years and interpreted based on the academic benefit to a majority of students and not on isolated cases.
- *The goal of the accountability system is student growth, not absolute achieve-*

ment scores. Because the focus is on student growth, there is no advantage for schools or classes with high-scoring students or disadvantage for schools with high mobility and absenteeism. Teachers mentioned a number of useful strategies in the area of instructional assistance for students as a result of the accountability system, which enhanced student learning. They included assistance in evaluating student abilities, the creation of special TAAS classes or tutoring for students who needed extra help, regrouping of students within classrooms according to specific skill deficits, and student gains in the area of writing.

- *A proactive effort is made to analyze and integrate multiple sources of standardized assessment data for use at the teacher, school, district, and state levels.* As noted earlier, there are multiple assessment strategies for grades 1-8 and separate tests for students with limited English proficiency. Results of these tests are used to calculate classroom and school indices and develop individual and school-based improvement plans.

Disadvantages

- *The student assessment measures do not attend to "complex cognitive performances and tasks."*[60] Despite an acknowledgment of the usefulness of test scores in focusing instruction and staff development, teachers emphasized the limitations of tests. For example, test scores reflect student learning only to the extent that children take them seriously and they are healthy, well rested, well fed, and emotionally settled the day of testing. Furthermore, even if test scores are accurate reflections of learning, they do not reflect attitudes toward learning, level of independence as learners, or a sense of efficacy as learners. These things are also important goals for teachers and yet can be overlooked with the emphasis on test data.

- *The DISD program involves a sophisticated system of assessments and statistical analysis that, in turn, requires a commitment in financial resources for the testing program and human resources to maintain and execute the extensive data analysis.* Linda Darling-Hammond in a review of the DISD system suggested few people in Dallas understand the system, limiting its value for teacher improvement. She recommended that the resources dedicated to accountability would be better spent on professional development and supporting well-qualified teachers.[61] In addition, Thum and Bryk[62] question the technical integrity of the two-stage regression model used by the DISD.

- *Students are tested multiple times with multiple instruments during each year, which may create too great an emphasis on assessment.* According to teachers, there are too many tests administered and this practice negatively impacts both students and teachers. For teachers, the focus on test results took the joy out of teaching, and for students, the testing program was stressful. The teachers also reported that most students take the testing program seriously although some do not, resulting in invalid test scores.

- *There is the potential for misuse or misinterpretation of data.* DISD has provided training in the proper use of the indices as one source of information and not the sole criterion of effectiveness. Roy Kemble, President of the Classroom Teachers of Dallas, said that "teachers want accountability, measurement is the issue."[63] From his perspective, the Dallas system has the potential to improve instruction at the classroom and school level or to blame teachers depending on the commitment of principals and teachers. His concern is the possible misuse of testing data to "hammer" teachers instead of using the data as a diagnostic tool for planning purposes.

What Are the Results of Implementation?

Mendro[64] reported a general increasing trend in achievement on the ITBS, the TAAS, the NAEP, and graduation rates. There also has been a decreasing trend in the dropout rate. Initially, there was a decrease in the percentage of students in honors courses in grades 7 to 8, but the percentage is again rising.

In addition, the indices have been used to evaluate the effectiveness of schools, principals, teachers, and program components. Based on longitudinal data, changes can be made to improve the educational experience, for children can be assessed and the impact of changes on test scores can be documented.

Teacher Perceptions

Teachers' views are mixed regarding the DISD student assessment program and its use in the teacher appraisal system. Teachers interviewed during a visit to Dallas seemed to agree that the system was fair, but they had concerns about the emphasis on assessment narrowing the curriculum and minimizing creativity.Teachers noted positive effects of the use of student assessment data in personnel evaluation. In the area of professional development, they identified the use of professional development to support teachers in the implementation of the TAAS objectives. For example, workshops were offered that focused on specific skill development. In terms of personnel decisions, teachers reported that no one had been fired as a result of the new teacher appraisal system but it was useful to "prod people along" who had weak test results.

Principal Perceptions

Principals who were interviewed thought the accountability system for teachers and schools using test data was fair because it factored out variables over which they had no control and predicted learning gains based on past performance at the individual level. One of the benefits of the testing program noted by one principal was that you could see the fruits of your labor in test results, if your interventions were successful.[65]

In terms of impact on personnel decisions, the principals confirmed the teachers' perception that the accountability system was not used for dismissal but was used in the remediation process or to make decisions about reassignment. In some cases, the principals reported that the use of test data helped to shift the focus in evaluation from stylistic issues to one of outcomes for students.

Conclusion

The Dallas Value-Added Accountability System is based on a sophisticated statistical model used to predict expected student growth at both classroom and school levels. Relevant factors affecting accountability are taken into account and controlled to address long standing concerns about fairness of such a system. While there continue to be questions about some aspects of the accountability system, most parties view it as a fair one. The use of student achievement data as an integral component in the teacher appraisal process was a radical shift for school personnel, but given the focus on improvement and professional development, teachers seem to think it has been implemented in a fair and reasonable manner.

IV.

ASSESSING TEACHER PERFORMANCE THROUGH REPEATED MEASURES OF STUDENT GAINS: THE TENNESSEE VALUE-ADDED ASSESSMENT SYSTEM

The Tennessee Value-Added Assessment System (TVAAS) is similar, in a number of respects, to the Dallas Accountability System in that it focuses on the outcomes of schooling and not the processes by which it is accomplished. It is a statistical model based on growth or gains in student achievement scores rather than fixed standards. Unlike the Dallas system, which compares student growth to the growth of other students with similar characteristics (e.g., gender and ethnicity), TVAAS compares each individual student's growth to his or her previous growth rate. That is, this year's gains for each student are compared to the gains made in previous years. Gains are expected to be similar, or possibly better, with more effective interventions. With TVAAS, each student serves as his or her own control for learning gains; it is assumed that the same potential for learning exists each year.

What Are the Purposes of the Accountability System, and How Was It Developed?

TVAAS was adopted as an important centerpiece of a comprehensive Tennessee education reform package, the Education Improvement Act,[66] passed in 1992. It resulted from a court decision finding school funding in Tennessee inequitable and, thus, unconstitutional. To gain support from the business community to raise the necessary new revenue for schools, the legislature needed an accountability system that linked student learning to classrooms and schools. Subsequently, a mixed model methodology developed by Bill Sanders at the University of Tennessee was selected to support the Tennessee Value-Added Assessment System.

The system Sanders developed for Tennessee, TVAAS, was designed to measure the "influence that school systems, schools, and teachers have on indicators of student learning."[67] Using TVAAS as a foundation, the legislature set school district performance standards for "demonstrating a mean gain for each academic subject within each grade greater than or equal to the national gain."[68] Also implied in the standards was the expectation that individual teachers would work toward a similar goal within their classrooms. In 1995, this expectation became explicit, and teacher effects on student learning became one of the data sources used for teacher evaluation.[69]

The primary purpose of TVAAS is to satisfy the accountability requirements of the Education Improvement Act. It provides information on the extent to which teachers, schools, and school systems facilitate learning gains for students as predicted by the previous three-year period. While the TVAAS information is not used as a sole indicator of effectiveness at any level, the information on schools and school systems is made public and creates pressure on schools to perform. It is expected to be used for the development of school and school district improvement plans. At the individual teacher level, the information is *not* public information and is shared only with the teacher and his or her supervisor. It is then used as one data source for the formulation of that teacher's professional development plan.

A secondary purpose of the TVAAS data is to serve as a feedback mechanism for curricular planning, program evaluation, and instructional adjustments with students of varying abilities. Test data in the annual reports are disaggregated by subject, grade level, and achievement levels, thus, giving schools information on how program modifications influence student achievement. With the breakdown of testing results by achievement levels, the reports can provide formative information on how modifications have affected all ability levels from low-achieving to high-achieving students. Teachers and administrators have used this information to support curricular reform and general school improvement. The data offer a measure of the success of educators as well as that of students.

Yet another purpose of the longitudinal database provided by TVAAS is educational research. With millions of records on student achievement over multiple years, analyses can be performed to examine the impact of various interventions at different grade levels, in different subjects, and even at different achievement levels. Several research initiatives have been undertaken both in-house and in collaboration with other researchers. One example of such work has been the examination of the "building change phenomenon."[70] This research has documented the diminished achievement of students in their first year at the next level of schooling (e.g., first year in middle school). Such research has the potential to help educators pinpoint inhibitors to academic growth and to identify those programs or strategies that sustain academic growth to create better learning environments for all students.

What Are the Student Assessment Strategies?

TVAAS uses data from an existing testing program operating statewide. It could, however, use other types of data if instrumentation were developed. The primary assessment instruments used by Tennessee at this time include the following:

- Tennessee Comprehensive Assessment Program for grades 2 through 8 in the subject areas of science, math, social studies, language arts, and reading[71]
- end-of-course tests in high school subjects (under development)
- a writing assessment.

The Tennessee Comprehensive Assessment Program (TCAP) is a combination of norm-referenced items TerraNova[72] and criterion-referenced items selected by teachers to reflect the Tennessee curricula. There is a high correlation between the norm-referenced and criterion-referenced items. Currently, end-of-course tests are being developed in the major subjects for grades 9 through 12.

How Does the Accountability System Work?

The sophisticated statistical methodology of the Tennessee Value-Added Assessment System offers a number of advantages over other approaches that attempt to isolate the effects of schooling on student achievement. The foundation of the system is longitudinal test data collected on every child in the Tennessee public schools. In most cases, several years of test results exist to use in estimating normal learning gains for any given year. Each individual student's previous academic progress then becomes the standard for future growth. From a statistical viewpoint, each student's past performance serves as a block for future performance to isolate factors that may affect learning; in essence, each student serves as his or her own control for expected growth.

Beginning in 1993, TVAAS provided compiled data on student academic gains to school systems in the form of a system report. The report summarized student gains for grades 3 through 8 in the five subjects of math, reading, language, science, and social studies. In addition, data were provided on the predicted growth gains for the system as a whole and average gains for the nation and state. Comparisons were then possible among a number of data points: predicted system gains, actual system gains, actual state gains, and actual national gains.

In 1994, school-level reports providing more narrowly focused school information were issued, and two years later, in 1996, individual teacher reports were distributed for the first time. Teacher reports contained similar information on average gains and predicted gains based on students assigned to that teacher, as well as average gains for the system, state, and nation. Predicted gains and actual gains were compared for individual teachers, but actual gains were not considered detectably different unless they were two standard errors of measurement above or below the predicted gains.[73] At the present time, system, school, and teacher reports are issued on an annual basis.

In addition to an analysis of student gains compared to predicted gains, the gain scores of students in a school or school system are compared to national norms. Deviations from the national norm gain are given for each grade and subject, thereby informing schools or systems whether their students are making comparable progress to other students in the nation. Schools and school systems are expected to achieve the national norm *gains* but not necessarily the national norm *scores*. "The cumulative average gain is the primary indicator by which success is measured,"[74] making growth the consistent focus of analysis.

In support of this approach of using student gains as a measure of effectiveness, Sanders and Horn analyzed the cumulative gains for schools across the state. They "found them to be unrelated to the racial composition of schools, the percentage of students receiving free and reduced-price lunches, or the mean achievement level of the school."[75] In other words, factors that are often associated with low achievement levels in absolute terms, such as race and poverty, are not associated with achievement gains. According to one observer, TVAAS has helped to shift the focus from absolute achievement levels to learning gains and has, thereby, helped to identify some real heroes in the Tennessee schools who have been overlooked in the past despite the notable learning gains they have effected with students.[76] And as a corollary, Wright, Sanders, and Horn have found that high achieving students, in absolute terms, often make minimal progress year to year.[77] According to the TVAAS research, the primary predictor of academic growth for students is not prior student achievement level, race, poverty, or class groupings; it is teacher effectiveness.[78]

While the primary emphasis of the accountability system is on student gains as measured by TCAP, other outcome measures used to assess the educational success of schools include:

- ACT results
- graduation rates
- student attendance rates
- promotion rates
- dropout rates.

Using these data, schools achieving state benchmarks in attendance and test gains are eligible for a $5000 award.

Safeguards

There are numerous safeguards built into TVAAS to enhance the fairness of the system:

- Estimates of school, school system, and teacher effectiveness are based on at least three years and no more than five years of assessment data.
- Schools, school systems, and teachers cannot be assessed solely on the basis of TVAAS.[79]
- A variety of media have been used to develop an understanding among educators about how to interpret and use TVAAS, including booklets, reports, workshops, presentations, and video presentations.
- A shrinkage estimate is used to determine the effects of a teacher, school, or school system on student gain. For teachers, this means, "all teachers are

assumed to be the average of their school system until the weight of the data pulls their specific estimates away from their school system's mean."[80] This tool protects teachers, schools, and school systems from short-term fluctuations in the test results.

- "Students must be tested annually with fresh, equivalent, nonredundant tests that exhibit a high level of reliability and validity."[81]
- Students identified by the school-based special education teams are excluded from the analysis of teacher effects. Virtually no students are excluded from the analysis of school effects.
- Students are not included in a teacher's assessment data unless they have been present 150 days in a given school year.[82]
- Test security is a high priority, and there are stringent sanctions for impropriety. TVAAS is also designed to "kick out" suspicious data.[83]
- Estimates of the impact of poverty, limited English, parents' level of education, etc. are unnecessary because they remain relatively constant for each child.

How Is the Accountability System Related to Teacher Evaluation?

TVAAS offers an estimate of the effects of a teacher, school, and school system on student achievement. While school and school system reports are public information, those for teachers are not. However, teacher reports are shared with teachers and their administrators. The Education Improvement Act requires the use of TVAAS data in the evaluation of teachers for whom it is available, but it cannot be the sole source of information. Under a new teacher evaluation framework, teachers work with their principals to develop a professional development plan linked to the school's improvement plan and reflecting the data from the TVAAS teacher report. Other options for teacher evaluation include cognitive coaching, teacher-devised professional improvement plans, cooperative teaching-related projects, and classroom observations.[84]

What Are the Advantages and Disadvantages of the Accountability System for Teacher Evaluation?

The Tennessee Value-Added Assessment System is a carefully conceptualized and highly technical statistical approach to measuring student gains. The resulting longitudinal database has provided an excellent research tool and useful data for examining teacher and school effects on student learning. Given its reliance on paper and pencil tests, however, reservations remain about its use for evaluation purposes. Here are some of the specific strengths and weaknesses.

Advantages

- *TVAAS is viewed statistically by experts as robust, fair, reliable, and valid.*[85] According to a review of TVAAS by Walberg and Paik, "Particularly strong points of TVAAS are the analysis of several years of data on teachers and an apparent system robustness despite ubiquitous missing data problems in longitudinal records."[86]
- *With a focus on improvement instead of achievement based on fixed standards, individual differences are accommodated.* Students are expected to grow and improve but not necessarily at the same rate or reach the same goal at the same time as other students. In some schools, students in math are regrouped frequently to focus instruction better on weaker skills or concepts. Teachers see many of these changes as positive. They now "accept kids where they are and then take them as far as possible."[87]
- *Teacher data provide a relatively simple measure of student progress and a teacher's ability to influence student learning outcomes.* Teachers acknowledge that TVAAS is one part of an effort to give the public some measure of their accomplishments and to make the schools as effective as possible. They found it overwhelming at first, but a comfort level is developing, as well as a sense that the system can be a positive tool.[88]
- *TCAP has good content validity because of the high degree of alignment with the Tennessee curricula.*[89] The TCAP achievement tests actually contain both norm-referenced items and criterion-referenced items that match the Tennessee curricula. There is also a high correlation between the criterion-referenced items and the norm-referenced items.[90] In terms of instruction, interviewed teachers stated that they now taught at a higher level in all subject areas and concentrated the teaching in a more curriculum-focused manner. One teacher reported, "There is not a lot of fluff, it's direct teaching all day long." [91] Another change has been in science where there has been an increased emphasis on hands-on activities to foster problem-solving skills reflected in the science curriculum and the TCAP test items.
- *Researchers have found a positive correlation between teacher effects as determined by TVAAS and subjective evaluations by supervisors.*[92] Research conducted as part of a feasibility study for TVAAS found a moderate relationship between quantitative measures of student gains and clinical judgments of their supervisors.

Disadvantages

- *TVAAS involves sophisticated statistical analyses that require a substantial programming effort and computing capability.* The University of Tennessee Value-Added Research and Assessment Center developed the software to handle the mixed model application for this large database. The center processes the information on a "UNIX workstation with 1 gigabyte of physical memory and 13 gigabytes of hard disk storage."[93] Many local school districts do not have the level of expertise or computing power to undertake an effort of this complexity.

- *There is the potential for misuse or misinterpretation of data.* There are concerns about the over-reliance on TVAAS as a sole, or even primary, indicator of success in teacher evaluation, the lack of training for administrators in its use and interpretation, and its narrow ability to measure the breadth of the enterprise called learning. There is variation in how different principals use the information, both positively and negatively.[94] In some cases, teachers noted that principals misused the data and unfairly blamed teachers for poor results. A number of educators confirmed that test results have been used as a basis for remediation and reassignment, but they have not been used in teacher dismissal.

- *Annual testing of students is a major investment of time, money, and human effort.* There also are concerns that the benefits do not justify the costs and that a comparable investment in professional development would be a better use of the money.[95] The actual cost of TVAAS in 1995 was 60 cents per student and TCAP was $3.59 per student. The combined cost of TVAAS and TCAP was less than one percent of the 1995 per pupil expenditures for students in Tennessee.[96]

- *TCAP provides a limited measure of the complex purposes of education.* According to critics like Darling-Hammond, it is questionable "what multiple-choice responses really measure . . . and they give no indication of the ability to apply information in a performance context."[97]

What Are the Results of Implementation?

Of primary importance is the impact of TVAAS on student learning, and Tennessee has been able to document increased student achievement for eighth grade students from 1991 to 1997.[98] Average student achievement as measured by TVAAS has increased in math, science, and language; however, social studies has remained constant and reading has decreased slightly (two scale score points). During the same time frame, there also have been increases in fourth grade math scores on the National Assessment of Educational Progress (NAEP).

In addition to tracking average student achievement, comparisons are made to national norm gains. According to data presented by the University of Tennessee Value-Added Research and Assessment Center, schools are making steady progress toward increasing their average gains as compared to the national gains. For example, 60.2 percent of the schools whose average gain in 1996 was 50 to 75 percent of the national average for language arts moved up to 75 to 100 percent of the national average gain in 1997.[99] Not only were they able to improve student gains relative to the students' past performance in language arts, but also they were able to close the gap between their students' gains and those of the nation as a whole.

Another area of impact has been in providing a focus for staff development. Test data are used to identify areas of insufficient instruction so that curricula or instructional strategies can be modified, for example in writing. Based on the results of test data, there has been intensive staff development in this area, and teachers report both subjective and objective measures of improvement. Many teachers seek out colleagues who have been highly effective in teaching the curriculum for ideas and suggestions. These teachers are sharing their work with other teachers through observations and workshops. The statewide Title I conference has served as a forum for presentations by teachers who have been particularly effective in enhancing student performance.[100]

Teacher Perspectives

Teachers acknowledge that the TVAAS results add pressure to the job, but "it keeps you on your toes." One teacher shared that with TVAAS, "one can't blame anyone else for student progress or lack thereof; it's the teacher's responsibility." It motivated her to stop and examine her practice. She is now more focused on academic gains. To her surprise, she has not encountered the negativity by other teachers she expected with the system.[101]

Principal Perspectives

TVAAS provides school- and teacher-based data that some principals find useful for school improvement. "Once you recognize what data does for you, if you've got the philosophy and willingness to change the school, you can drastically affect the learning of individual students. It's that simple."[102] Another principal noted that the information enhances data-driven decision-making, which yields good gains and a sense of school pride. The feedback helps to focus everyone on achievement and improves performance.

Rick Privette, principal at Carver Elementary School in East Knox County, Tennessee, says that he tries to make the sharing of TVAAS data with teachers non-threatening, and he balances it with professional judgment. He examines the data for patterns of results and if necessary, addresses needed improvements in the annual development plan. He emphasizes that test results are not used as the sole means of teacher evaluation.[103]

Conclusion

Sanders and Horn have expressed the goal of providing educators with information that will give direction for improving student academic gain, enabling students to receive more equal opportunity regardless of where they go to school.[104] Properly conducted and analyzed test results have the potential to provide one set of lenses for making sense of the effects of schooling on students. Results from TVAAS suggest that students in Tennessee are doing better on TCAP, and teachers report more focused instruction in classrooms, but it remains to be seen whether this progress translates into better school experiences for all children.

As schools and policy makers pursue progressively better approaches to ensuring quality education for students, TVAAS distinguishes itself by shifting the focus from fixed standards to academic progress and truly individualizing discussions of student progress. Sanders and Horn spoke to these moral obligations to students when they stated:

> TVAAS was developed on the premise that society has a right to expect that schools will provide students with the opportunity for academic gain regardless of the level at which the students enter the educational venue. In other words, all students can and should learn commensurate with their abilities.[105]

V.

ASSESSING TEACHER PERFORMANCE WITH STUDENT WORK: THE OREGON TEACHER WORK SAMPLE METHODOLOGY

Teaching is far from a fine science; indeed, the process of helping others learn (a.k.a. teaching) can be fairly characterized as a highly complex undertaking. The ambitious goal of the Oregon Teacher Work Sample Methodology (TWSM) is to find better ways to assess the complexities of teaching and its connections to student learning. We selected TWSM to review as one model for teacher evaluation because of its potential to provide systematic ways and means of assessing real samples of teacher work—despite the inherent difficulty in doing so.

What Are the Purposes of the Accountability System, and How Was It Developed?

Del Schalock, one of the key developers of the TWSM, alluded to the importance of relating teaching to learning results when he stated that "the underpinning of medicine is healing, not the methods the physicians use."[106] The focus for improvement and accountability in this medical analogy is on what happens as a result of the intervention, and far less on the process of the intervention itself. Likewise, as reflected in the TWSM, the explicit purpose of teaching and, consequently, teacher evaluation, is to focus on the effects of teaching and to provide a direct link between teaching and learning.

The TWSM process is designed to foster both formative and summative teacher reflection and self-evaluation, both of which are "important components of teachers' professional development. It focuses teachers on pupil learning as the fundamental purpose and criterion of good teaching."[107] Simply put, TWSM is built upon the "assumption that the job of teaching is 'are kids making progress?'"[108]

The TWSM is an outgrowth of educational reform in Oregon. In 1991, the

Oregon Legislature passed an educational reform statute that required schooling to be "extensively restructured so that all students would meet high standards."[109] Consistent with this legislative mandate, the Oregon Teacher Standards and Practices Commission instituted a redesign of teacher licensure requirements to reflect a standards-based model of schooling. "In Oregon, and particularly at Western [Western Oregon University], an appraisal method has been developed that is meaningful to emerging teachers...and grounded in the complex reality of what teachers do."[110] This appraisal method has come to be known as *teacher work sample methodology* (TWSM)."

The vast majority of the TWSM development to date has been with pre-service teachers, used to assess their teaching competencies as part of initial teacher licensure. Nonetheless, the TWSM approach is reflective of many teacher evaluation systems that include portfolios, dossiers, or other samples of teacher work. Kenneth Wolf and colleagues described teaching portfolios as "increasingly popular tools for both evaluation and professional development," perhaps due to their authentic nature.[111] Del Schalock, Mark Schalock, and Andrew McConney, developers and researchers of the Oregon TWSM, refer to this assessment process as "close to a teacher's work . . ."[112]

> When complete, a teacher's work sample can be viewed as a compact, delimited teacher portfolio, with some important differences . . . For example, a portfolio typically represents a fairly long span of time (e.g., an entire school year, with supporting materials from previous years), whereas a teacher work sample brings a fine focus to a shorter period of teaching and learning. More important, whereas a teacher portfolio can include a broad representation of a teacher's work and professional development, TWSM is designed to focus teachers on [selected] issues . . .[113]

> The goal of the Teacher Effectiveness Project at Western Oregon University is to create a fully developed, validated and reliable Teacher Work Sample Methodology (TWSM) that provides a conceptual framework with which teachers and teacher development programs (preservice and inservice) can think about, learn about, practice, and demonstrate their proficiencies along a number of dimensions related to schools. TWSM is a methodology designed to serve training and research functions, as well as evaluation and licensure functions.[114]

Given the intent to develop TWSM as a reliable and valid teacher evaluation approach that is appropriate for multiple purposes, including formative and summative evaluation, we will briefly examine the evidence related to these technical attributes. Then, we will review how the TWSM system works.

Reliability Evidence

A key question to be answered is whether the methodology produces consistent results. The developers were aware that work sample products and performance must be judged consistently across raters. In their efforts to answer this thorny question, they checked for levels of agreement between college and school supervisor ratings provided around a student teacher's work sample implementation (perfor-

---

Table 1

Validation Evidence Supporting the Oregon TWSM

Type of Validation	Evidence Gathered by Developers
• *Face validity*—the *appearance*, relevance, and clarity of the scoring guides used to rate performance and product quality with TWSM	Feedback from teacher focus groups indicated that they generally viewed the TWSM as reasonable and reflective of "what teachers do." Thus, on its face, the process appears to be reasonable.
• *Content validity*—the degree to which the TWSM aligns with descriptions of what teachers do and the domains of effective teacher knowledge and skills	Analyses were conducted to compare the proficiencies measured by the TWSM with other accepted frameworks of what effective teaching involves. The results of these comparative analyses yielded good matches with various frameworks, including Scriven's *Duties of The Teacher (DOTT)*,[117] Educational Testing Service,[118] and the National Board for Professional Teaching Standards.[119]
• *Construct validity*—the degree to which the TWSM aligns with the philosophy of teaching and learning embodied in the policies of the state's teacher licensing agency and, more broadly, with the state's design for schooling[120]	The TWSM is designed to maintain a focus on student learning as the central purpose and outcome of teaching. In an effort to measure this desired teaching-learning connection, regression analyses (conducted using teacher-reported student learning measures) indicated that teacher work sample measures accounted for between 24.5 percent (grades 3-5) and 59.5 percent (grades 6-8) of the variance observed in student learning. These data tend to suggest that what teachers do has a measurable influence on student learning.

mance in the classroom). The findings of this study were encouraging, with inter-rater agreement ranging from 81 to 98 percent.[115]

Validity Evidence

The developers considered various forms of validation evidence (i.e., the degree to which the TWSM measures what it purports to measure) with the results summarized in Table 1.[116]

In summarizing the technical development of the TWSM, the developers noted the following:

> Content (face) and construct validity do not appear to be a problem for most of the measures obtained through TWSM *so long as one does not wish to draw inferences about performance or effectiveness of a teacher beyond the sample of teaching and learning represented in a particular sample of work.* If one wishes to make such inferences and there is a strong tendency to do so, then the technical issues involved become as much a matter of ensuring an adequate sample of teaching contexts and learning outcomes pursued as they do of ensuring the adequacy of measures used.[121]

While the validation evidence for TWSM is encouraging, it is important to note that predictive validity—the degree to which results generated through the TWSM can forecast the effectiveness of practicing teachers—as yet has not been established.[122] Thus, while the methodology is promising, its application—and, indeed, the application of any high stakes teacher evaluation system—needs to be underpinned with evidence that it can accurately differentiate performance.

What Are the Student Assessment Strategies?

The TWSM relies heavily on authentic classroom assessment to document student learning. Using teacher-made tests, the TWSM employs a gain score measure to calculate student learning and to infer the teacher's influence on the learning. Starting with pre-test scores for all students in a classroom,

> the teacher calculates a *percentage correct* score for each student. Then, the teacher a) tabulates the range of preinstructional scores, b) sorts the scores into high, middle, and low scoring groups, and c) calculates the mean scores for each of the groups as well as for the class as a whole. Using these preinstructional data as a point of departure, the teacher can then proceed to refine them to bring *a level of standardization* to the teacher-designed and curriculum-aligned measures of pupil learning used. This is done by calculating an Index of Pupil Growth (IPG) score for each pupil. The IPG is a simple metric devised by [Jason] Millman[123] to show the percentage of potential growth each pupil actually achieved.

The metric is calculated as follows:

$$\frac{(\text{Post \% correct}) - (\text{Pre \% correct})}{(100\% - \text{Pre \% correct})}$$

Multiplying this metric by 100 results in a score that can range from −100 to +100, where a negative number represents a lower score on the posttest than on the pretest, 0 represents a no gain score on the posttest, and +100 represents a perfect score on the posttest regardless of pretest performance. A negative score is rare, with most scores falling in the +30 to +80 range.[124]

How Does the Accountability System Work?

TWSM is anchored in an "outcome-based and context-dependent" theory of teacher effectiveness.[125] It is designed to require teachers (and, by extension, their evaluators) to focus on and bring the following issues into alignment:

- What are the learning outcomes I want *my* students to accomplish?
- What activities and instructional methodologies are appropriate or necessary for *these* students to achieve *these* outcomes?
- What resources and how much time do I need to implement these activities or methodologies?
- What assessment activities or methodologies are appropriate for these students and these outcomes when using these instructional methodologies?
- How successful was I at helping my students achieve the outcomes desired? What went right?
- What went wrong? Why?[126]

Implementation Procedures

"As an approach to measurement, TWSM has been designed to portray the learning progress of pupils on outcomes desired by a teacher and taught by a teacher over a sufficiently long period of time for appreciable progress in learning to occur."[127] This means TWSM requires that teachers document an extended sample of their work. The work sample would include descriptions of the context of the teaching and learning, desired learning outcomes, instructional plans and resources, assessments used, and, finally, the growth in learning achieved by students. Further, the process requires teachers (and prospective teachers) "to assess and reflect on their own performance in terms of the learning achieved by each of their students..."[128] Thus, a vital aspect of the TWSM is intended to go beyond the teaching-learning processes and products; it is designed to encourage—even require—significant reflection on the work as the teacher continuously attempts to improve the art and science of teaching.

"Simply put, TWSM requires teachers to think about, develop, implement, document, and present samples of their work as evidence of their effectiveness."[129] A central feature of this process is documenting evidence of student progress in learning. As an authentic and applied teacher performance appraisal measure, teachers are asked to implement the following nine steps:

1. Define the sample of teaching and learning to be described
2. Identify learning outcomes to be accomplished within the work to be sampled
3. Assess the learning status of students prior to instruction with respect to the postinstruction outcomes
4. Align instruction and assessment with outcomes to be accomplished
5. Describe the context in which teaching and learning are to occur
6. Adapt outcomes desired, and related plans for instruction and assessment, to accommodate the demands of the teaching-learning context
7. Implement a developmentally and contextually appropriate instructional plan
8. *Assess the postinstructional accomplishments of learners and calculate on a student-by-student basis the growth in learning achieved*
9. Summarize, interpret, and reflect on student learning growth and other assessment information.

Step 8 is italicized "to emphasize that TWSM makes explicit to all constituencies the inclusion and prominence of students' learning gains in the definition of 'teacher effectiveness.'"[130]

Illustration of how the TWSM works. How are these concepts and the scoring rubric applied in the assessment of a teacher's work? As depicted in Table 2, the outline of the key components drawn from an actual elementary school life science work sample might serve to illustrate this process.[131]

How Is the Accountability System Related to Teacher Evaluation?

The TWSM is a highly structured and fairly complex assessment process. Nonetheless, it is viewed as only one among several information sources to be used in making judgments about teacher effectiveness. "Teacher work sample methodology is an extended applied performance assessment comprising multiple performance tasks. For prospective teachers...the results of this assessment are used as one source of evidence in gauging their attainment of teaching proficiencies at specified benchmarks..."[132] Although the successful completion of at least two teacher work samples is required for initial licensure in Oregon, the work sample assessment "is only one line of evidence used in making a licensure decision."[133] As with all other teacher evaluation systems we consider in this book, multiple measures of teacher performance (e.g., standardized achievement test results, traditional classroom observations) would be required.

Table 2	
Elementary Life Science "Spiders" Work Sample	
Key Components in Work Sample	**Details Provided**
Background information	• Description of the school and classroom • Student demographic information
Lesson outline	• Rationale for the lesson unit • Learning goals and objectives • Graphic organizer for the lesson sequence • Lesson plan details (e.g., materials, instructional sequence, time estimate) • Materials to be used in the lesson
Student assessment plan	• Pre- and post-assessment procedures • Instruction and assessment alignment matrix • Scoring guide for student work
Work sample assessment results	• Samples of student work • Net learning gains (post-assessment - pre-assessment = learning gains) by individual students • Net learning gains by students grouped in clusters
Teacher reflection	• Assessment analysis-narrative summary and review of student learning results • Reflective essay-narrative discussion of what went right, what went wrong, and how to improve in future lessons

What Are the Advantages and Disadvantages of the Accountability System for Teacher Evaluation?

In our effort to discern noted (or potential) strengths and weaknesses of the Oregon TWSM, we reviewed research findings published by the TWSM development team as well as critiques of the process by noted educational researchers with an interest in teacher evaluation.[134] Also, we interviewed program developers, university faculty who employ the system, and teacher candidates who have been evaluated based on the TWSM. The key advantages and disadvantages are described below.

Advantages

- *It offers a reasonable method for naturally linking teaching with learning.* "From our viewpoint, there are as many reasons for optimism about TWSM as an approach to measurement as there are reasons for concern.... The first of these is the reasonableness of the methodology from the perspective of teachers, parents, and school administrators, school board members, and the public at large. It anchors to the criterion of ultimate interest (pupil learning), it links pupil learning to teacher work and the realities of the context in which teaching and learning occur, it ensures that measures of pupil learning are connected to what is taught and what pupils are expected to learn, and it provides information about the performance and characteristics of teachers assumed to be related to pupil learning."[135]
- *The TWSM process focuses directly on the connection between teacher behavior and student learning.* "TWSM is all about teacher learning and student learning, not comparison across groups. It is a homemade measure of teacher work and student work that demonstrates student learning."[136] "Using TWSM, teachers show whether they can develop and employ respectable performance assessments. In high-stakes evaluations, the state and school districts could consider such self-assessment evidence along with a wide range of other more objectively gathered information."[137]
- *TWSM considers the context of teaching as a major component of teacher evaluation.* "The TWSM allows the opportunity to consider the context of teaching and learning, for example, analysis of groups and reflection on the setting. It helps explain learning gains (or the lack thereof). Also it helps target the learning needs of all students."[138]
- *It helps focus the teacher's work on good instruction.* The discussion in a supervisor-teacher meeting can (and should) focus on student learning—the essence of good teaching.
- *It provides alignment between the goals and practice of teaching.* As noted by one teacher we interviewed, "The TWSM helps align the goals of teaching with actual teaching."[139] "The major advantage of enacting state policies to require the use of work samples is the increased focus on improving and assessing pupil achievement gains."[140]
- *The teaching-learning connection embeds assessment in daily teaching.* "It informs teacher work and informs students of where they are and where they need to go. It builds capacity to manage one's own learning."[141]
- *It serves as a valuable tool for formative assessment of teachers.* TWSM is viewed as a way to know what teachers know and are able to do, and as a vehicle to guide professional development.
- *It encourages teacher reflection and action research.* One of the major bene-

fits of TWSM is that it encourages, even requires, reflection by the teacher on the craft of teaching. "My improvement from beginning to end is amazing. [The process] caused me to think about things I would never have thought about."[142] It provides an opportunity to use "hand-made assessments, provide instruction, then look at the results and reflect on what happened."[143] As Linda Darling-Hammond noted, "there is value in an approach to teacher evaluation that points practitioners to the careful evaluation of practices, contexts, and outcomes, including the systematic consideration of student and teacher work. I have no doubt that this encourages teachers to reflect on their work in ways that are extremely productive for developing diagnostic habits of thinking as well as specific practices."[144]

Disadvantages

- *It is difficult to provide statistical defensibility of applied performance measures such as TWSM.* Traditional measures of reliability and validity (as discussed earlier) are serious concerns in the use of applied performance measures such as Oregon's TWSM. The loosely structured, non-standardized, student assessment process inherent in the TWSM makes comparability, consistency, and defensibility serious challenges to overcome.

- *TWSM places a premium on quality teacher-developed measures of student learning—a difficult task to achieve in practice.* "One primary concern is the quality of the pre- and posttests constructed by teachers to assess their pupils' learning."[145] "If assessments are crummy or are not aligned with the curriculum, then the methodology won't demonstrate what was taught."[146]

- *There is an obvious difficulty in achieving inter-rater reliability with complex samples of teaching.* Despite the encouraging inter-rater agreement results summarized earlier in the chapter, this issue will continue to be a challenge in successfully implementing TWSM-type teacher evaluation strategies. A partial solution to this dilemma may lie in better design of methods for scoring teacher work samples and measuring student learning gains. Another potential solution is better training for evaluators. Reliability concerns, however, are inherent in analyses of qualitative data sources.

- *The ability to assess certain aspects of teaching can dictate what is taught.* The ease and availability of selected assessment strategies has the potential to limit curriculum and instruction in undesirable ways. "*What* can be assessed can determine the goals and objectives—instruction—assessment—student learning cycle. It's important to include more than knowledge acquisition; include concept acquisition and application."[147] It is not clear "to what extent teachers select easy-to-meet objectives or teach narrowly to the specific posttest items. Although it is important to align objectives, instruction, and assessment to one another, it also is important that the objectives themselves be meaningful and worthwhile."[148]

- *The pre-assessment strategies required in the TWSM can be an unnecessary limiting factor.* "Once goals and objectives, and then preassessments, are set,

[one] can feel confined to teach that material, even when different learning needs arise. There is a need for flexibility."[149]

- *Instructional design, development, delivery, and assessment using TWSM requires a significant time commitment.* Simply put, "work samples are a lot of work."[150] This is true not only for the teacher, but also for the administrator who is reviewing the work samples and providing feedback on the teacher's performance.
- *Although the TWSM may provide an authentic and in-depth assessment of a given work sample of a teacher, it is too narrow and uncontrolled for making high stakes decisions.* "It provides too few points to help the student teacher monitor his or her pupils' progress during an instruction unit. As implemented so far, it considers only a small amount of the student teacher's instruction."[151] "The assessments are not standardized or controlled. Teachers greatly influence what they assess and at what level of performance."[152]
- *Assessment systems using gain scores have inherent measurement problems.* "The IPG [Index of Pupil Growth] is the index used to measure pupil learning gains. It is clear, however, that raw gain scores do not provide a direct indication of the unique contribution a teacher makes to the gains. Other factors such as pupils' prior knowledge, socioeconomic status, student language proficiency, classroom resources, and the like also can influence pupil learning gains."[153]

What Are the Results of Implementation?

With some precautionary notes, the findings to date regarding the use of the Oregon TWSM are encouraging. The connection between effective teaching and student learning inherent in the TWSM is logical and would be a natural outgrowth of teacher work. As one teacher candidate stated, "When I look at what my students are learning, it changes what I am doing and where I am going in my professional development to meet the needs of students."[154] The development of this approach, however, should be viewed with some caution within the context of assessing teacher performance. Remember that the studies conducted have been almost exclusively with aspiring teachers, not practicing teachers. Likewise, the focus of the TWSM has been on evaluating the worthiness of teacher candidates entering the teaching field, not on evaluating the effectiveness of practicing teachers.

Conclusion

As noted throughout this chapter, the Oregon Teacher Work Sample Methodology has received mixed reviews as a useful teacher evaluation method. Obviously, there still is work to be done on the work sample methodology. There are both significant technical and practical concerns to be addressed if the process is to receive widespread application. Nonetheless, the potential value of the TWSM, or derivations thereof, clearly exists. We think the following selection of comments—some from TWSM developers, some from critics of the process—tends to offer a summary reflection on the current state-of-the-art of this still-emerging approach for linking naturalistic teacher work with student learning.

- "The Western Oregon teacher effectiveness research reflects a growing and appropriate consensus that teacher evaluation should focus squarely on improving pupil achievement."[155]
- "Of equal importance from the perspective of teachers, we believe the methodology and its various applications stand to enhance the professionalization of teaching. Pupil learning is, always has been and must continue to be the professional touchstone for teachers, and TWSM provides a means for this linkage to be made meaningfully and defensibly."[156]
- "Ironically, TWSM, for all its limitations, is one of the best available teacher evaluation techniques. It is more systematic and useful for assessing teacher effectiveness based on pupil outcome data than are most other practices of teacher evaluation. This is a sobering commentary on the state of teacher evaluation."[157]
- "The Oregon work sampling approach has this to commend it: It actually looks at teaching, and it does so in the context of teachers' goals, classroom contexts, and student learning, measured in ways that attempt to link learning to the educational goals being sought. In these respects, it stands head and shoulders above…other approaches…as a means for providing sound evaluations of teaching that might also be useful in helping teachers improve."[158]

VI.

ASSESSING TEACHER PERFORMANCE IN A STANDARDS-BASED ENVIRONMENT: THE THOMPSON, COLORADO, SCHOOL DISTRICT

The teacher evaluation program of Colorado's Thompson School District, in technical terms, is the least sophisticated of the four case studies that we have chosen to highlight. While the evaluation system is less sophisticated in technical design, it does reflect a high degree of political sophistication (e.g., gaining broad-based school and community support for holding teachers accountable for student performance). It does not have the statistical base that supports the Tennessee and Dallas gain score efforts, nor does it have the careful research record that has been amassed for the Oregon work samples project. Rather, we selected it as one of the case studies *because* of its simplicity. While each of the other teacher evaluation models offers distinct methodological advantages in connecting teacher performance to student performance, the Thompson experience might be considered more as a starting point for many schools and school districts: it is straightforward, easy to understand, and was implemented within the district's technical and fiscal capacity.

What Are the Purposes of the Accountability System, and How Was It Developed?

In many respects, the Thompson R2-J School District in Loveland, Colorado, is like many of America's school districts: it has limited financial means but unlimited aspirations for its students. Thompson, located approximately 50 miles north of Denver and within a few miles of Rocky Mountain National Park, is a district of 28 schools with approximately 14,200 students. The 1998-99 annual per pupil expenditure in the district was approximately $4600, low within Colorado (173rd out of 176) and certainly low by comparison with national averages. With this comparatively low budget, teacher salaries, too, were lower than those in many surrounding districts. Despite the financial limits of the district, students historically have performed somewhat higher than students in communities with comparable SES levels; nonetheless, there was a belief within the Loveland educational community—including among parents, school board members, administrators, and teachers—that students could do better.

Designing the Evaluation System

Given this scenario, in 1993 the school board began investigating ways and means of attracting and retaining well qualified teachers and of increasing student achievement. With strong community support and encouragement, the initial direction taken in addressing these dual challenges was to consider a teacher pay-for-performance program.

Work began in the 1993-94 school year with the creation of a "Performance Pay Design Committee," with members jointly selected by the school district administration and the local NEA affiliate. Shortly after its formation, the committee solicited input from the business community regarding performance pay. Next, focus group meetings were conducted with stakeholder groups in an effort to understand what the greater community desired from its schools. Additionally, the committee surveyed teachers and parents in every school to gather their perceptions on how to improve the schools. Based on the findings from this year-long planning effort and with strong community support, the committee shifted away from merely considering pay for performance to a more systemic school improvement process.

Beginning with the 1994-95 school year, the committee continued work with its broadened school improvement mission, with a specific focus on designing an effective performance assessment system. The committee invested considerable effort into designing teacher job performance standards and then into developing implementation procedures for the evaluation system. Next, the draft evaluation system was submitted to independent reviewers. Following revisions suggested from the draft review, the committee presented the teacher standards and evaluation system to teachers and administrators for their consideration.

Piloting and Staff Development

A two-year pilot process began the following academic year, with major revisions made after evaluation of the first year's implementation and more minor modifications made after the second. At the completion of this extensive four-year planning, development, and piloting sequence, the school board was ready to implement the new standards-based teacher evaluation system district-wide.

As the school district moved toward full implementation, administrator and teacher training was undertaken. At the beginning of the 1997-98 school year, all school administrators participated in a three-day training program designed to introduce the new system and to build technical skills in areas related to school improvement and teacher evaluation. The skill building components for supervisors included the following:

- role playing to provide hands-on experience with the new evaluation system
- conducting effective pre- and post-observation conferences
- improving supervision style
- supporting data-driven instruction
- monitoring performance in a standards-based teacher evaluation system
- coaching.

Following the administrator training, a training-the-trainers model was used to introduce the system fully to the district's teachers. Teacher leaders representing all schools were brought to training sessions on the new system. According to John Stewart, the assistant superintendent and one of the key architects of the evaluation system, these training sessions were not focused solely on the technical aspects of the system: attention was also devoted in the teacher training to "eliminating worst fears and debugging rumors."[159] Finally, the teacher leaders and principals delivered training to all teachers in each building, and the new teacher evaluation system was launched.

What Are the Student Assessment Strategies?

The evaluation system involves a gain score approach to student assessment that incorporates both standardized and more informal measures of student performance. Beginning in kindergarten and extending through 12th grade, a wide array of both standardized and informal measures are used to assess student performance. Operationally, the student performance assessments can be grouped into four categories[160]:

- norm-referenced tests—e.g., Iowa Test of Basic Skills, PSAT, and SAT
- state standards assessment—Colorado State Assessment Program (CSAP) fourth, seventh, and tenth grade tests aligned with Colorado's content standards
- criterion-referenced tests—e.g., Scholastic End-of-Year tests, reading or math level tests, science process skills tests, and performance-based proficiency tests
- classroom assessments—teacher-made classroom assessments, including multiple choice, essay, performance tasks, demonstrations, and student portfolios.

How Does the Teacher Evaluation System Work?

Early in the evaluation development process[161] the Thompson Board of Education adopted the belief statement below to guide the expectations, design, and implementation of the teacher evaluation system. It was consistent with the Colorado

State Legislature's requirement that each school district in the state develop a written instrument for evaluating certified school district staff members.[162]

> The Board of Education, administration, staff and parents are committed to providing and maintaining the best possible education for our students. An important indicator of an excellent educational program is the competence and professionalism of the district's instructional staff. The district recognizes that the instructional process is extremely complex, and the appraisal of the school professional's performance is a challenging endeavor *but critical to the educational goals, achievement,* and well-being of our students. [*emphasis added*]

In addition to this overarching belief statement, the Board adopted several specific beliefs regarding the evaluation system, the first of which reads, "The School Professional Evaluation and Supervision Process should focus on the enhancement of student achievement and well-being." Thus, the Thompson School District Professional Evaluation System is squarely focused on the district's overarching goals: "to increase student achievement and well-being."[163]

Under the umbrella of increasing student achievement and well-being,[164] the key components in the evaluation system are designed to connect teacher and student expectations logically and are fairly straightforward:

- Identification of teacher performance standards
- Implementation of the Thompson standards and evaluation system
- Connection of evaluation results to professional development.

Teacher Performance Standards

The evaluation system begins with the identification of ten teacher professional standards[165] for which all teachers are held accountable and against which their performance is measured. These ten teacher professional standards include, among others, expectations such as "demonstrates the basic components of effective instruction,…designs and implements instruction to meet the unique needs of students," and "communicates with students [and] families…concerning student academic and behavioral progress." While these standards imply the connection between teacher performance and student learning, it is Standard 3 that makes this expectation explicit:

> The school professional is responsible for increasing the probability of advancing student achievement.[166]

While the phrase *increasing the probability of advancing student achievement* may be somewhat cushioned and coded language, the expectation is clear: teachers and other educational professionals will be held accountable for student learning.

Evaluation Implementation Procedures

The evaluation system links directly to student achievement—but only as one factor in the teacher's performance review. In addition to direct measures of student learning, other sources include formal and informal observations, self-evaluation, and reviews of artifacts related to job performance. This multiple source data collection process culminates in a summative evaluation conference, during which judgments are made regarding the teacher's performance in the evaluation cycle, based on the cumulative evidence.

Professional Development

In addition to assessing performance against the ten teacher professional standards, the summative evaluation conference provides an opportunity to connect the teacher's performance to her or his professional development needs in the upcoming evaluation cycle. Specifically, five different developmental stages for teachers have been identified and incorporated into the evaluation system[167]:

1. A *probationary evaluation* is used with teachers who are new to the district, to complete an induction process that aligns performance with the district's teaching standards.
2. A *performance review* process is used annually to assess formally whether teachers on a multi-year cycle continue to meet district performance standards.
3. A *school professional evaluation* allows for evaluator-directed or collaborative goal-setting during a one- or two-year evaluation cycle.
4. A *self-directed school professional evaluation* is an advanced goal-setting process that allows teachers who have shown acceptable or commendable performance an opportunity to set professional goals over a three- to five-year cycle.
5. An *improvement evaluation* emphasizes remediation for teachers beyond the probationary levels who are not meeting district standards; it is used as a tool in making employment decisions.

Ultimately, the entire standards-based evaluation system, from professional standards to performance assessment to professional growth and improvement, is predicated on improving student achievement.

How Is the Accountability System Related to Teacher Evaluation?

As noted earlier, the basic approach to assessing gain scores can be expressed as follows:

student's ending achievement level – beginning achievement level = gain score

Don Saul, the superintendent of schools, stated the assessment strategy this way: "We have to measure student growth, not snapshots with different cohorts. We focus on a value-added perspective."[168]

In this gain score environment, the following sequence of events unfolds: (a) the student's baseline performance is determined, (b) the teacher provides "data-driven" instruction, and (c) the student's post-instruction performance is assessed. The framework for the "data-driven" instruction process[169] is cyclical and includes the following steps:

1. Start with *content standards*.
2. Create/find *assessment* aligned to content standards.
3. Assess for *diagnostic* purposes.
4. Analyze the *data*.
5. Identify the *learning styles* of students.
6. Plan for a variety of *teaching/learning strategies* and environments.
7. Implement the *instruction*. Monitor and adjust as needed.
8. *Administer* assessment for evaluation.

In essence, benchmarks for student learning goals are set with standardized tests and informal assessments used to measure performance.

Assessment in the above data-driven instruction process is played out with guidance from the district regarding which of the previously identified tests listed above to use and when to use them. The classroom teacher, however, has considerable latitude in deciding how and when to use classroom assessments as part of student performance assessment, provided that efforts are made to utilize a variety of assessment instruments both prior to instruction for planning purposes and as summative evaluations for documentation of student progress.

What Are the Advantages and Disadvantages of the Accountability System for Teacher Evaluation?

In an effort to assess the advantages and disadvantages in a standards-based teacher evaluation program, we interviewed a cross-section of Thompson's educational community. Additionally, we reviewed the evaluation system documents and considered design elements and results of the program. The following is a summary of these findings.

Advantages

- *There is a clearer focus on student learning needs.* "We focus more on what students need to learn, not covering the curriculum."[170] "If you look at data-driven student learning, you get better results than going with what the publisher says the next chapter should be.... Teachers are employing research-based instruction."[171]

 46

- *The standards-based approach to evaluation is professionalizing.* "Evaluation systems historically have talked process, not outcomes. The primary advantage is that you get people to re-examine their beliefs about what is good for children."[172] "[There is an] assumption that professionals have a certain level of knowledge and that changes can be made in response to student achievement."[173]
- *The evaluation system provides a customer focus.* "Students are the customers, parents and community are key stakeholders."[174]
- *The evaluation system is motivating to teachers.* "[The evaluation system] makes teachers feel better…when you see the results, you know you've helped kids."[175]
- *Teacher collegiality is encouraged.* "It has given a lot more collegiality in professional development."[176] "You can't do this without sharing [thus, some of the isolation of teaching is removed]."[177] [The evaluation system] "increases quality interactions among professionals: principal-to-teacher and teacher-to-teacher."[178]
- *The standards for evaluation are clearer.* "It is clear what teachers are being evaluated on and takes away a lot of the subjectivity."[179]
- *Teacher performance improvement is emphasized.* "If we aren't encouraging low performing employees to improve, we're accepting a level of mediocrity."[180] "[In] data-driven—or data-influenced—decision making we can find what some of our best practices are to improve student achievement and replicate them."[181]
- *Staff development is more directly connected to student learning needs.* "If you look at data driven staff development, you increase the probability of improving student learning."[182]

Disadvantages

- *This evaluation approach allows for significant variability in implementation.* "The system is only as good as the practitioner."[183]
- *The evaluation system can stifle risk taking and creativity.* "My major concern is that teachers will interpret the importance of test performance in a 'drill and kill' instructional approach that is overly narrow. We need a moderate approach."[184]
- *The multi-tiered student assessment system lacks stringent statistical controls.* "[There is] confusion about the multiple assessments that can be used to measure student learning."[185] "We have a primitive database from which to work with value-added impact of teaching. Knowledge of educational effectiveness is limited in being able to account for all learning factors."[186]
- *Clear-cut and comparable measures of student improvement are difficult to obtain.* "[It is] difficult to determine the vehicle to measure student growth that is acceptable by teachers, administrators, and the community.'[187]
- *The system requires a significant time commitment to student assessment.* "When doing a lot of student assessment, what gives is teaching time. Teacher

scheduling and planning are complicated by so much testing."[188] "[The evaluation system requires] more time in testing, more research to get the scores, more time in developing ways to assess."[189]

- *Evaluating teachers based on student achievement is threatening.* "It's scary to a lot of teachers to be evaluated on how our students achieve."[190] "[There are] very long-standing concerns of elements outside of school that influence student learning."[191]
- *Public reporting of test results is stressful.* "There is pressure from public reporting [of] test results..."[192] "[There is] stress in getting your scores and reading them in the paper the same night."[193]
- *The budget impact is substantial.* "There is a huge budgetary impact to focus on improving student test scores."[194]
- *In an incentive performance pay plan, there is a financial penalty for poor results.* "[There is] the fear that my students, for varying reasons, don't score well next year. If a teacher gets a poor evaluation, [he or she is] frozen on the salary schedule and not allowed to take part in performance pay."[195]

What Are the Results of Implementation?

One clear and significant disadvantage inherent in a standards-based teacher evaluation system is the difficulty in directly and precisely attributing student performance to teacher performance. Nonetheless, when the Thompson experience is viewed in its totality, there is substantial evidence that the system is succeeding. While the impact of a given teacher's influence on student learning can only be approximated, the school district can definitively point to the overall outcome of the experience: student learning as measured by standardized test scores is increasing.

As evidence of the demonstrated increase in student performance, school officials point to the progress of Thompson students on the Colorado State Assessment Program (CSAP). In 1997, 65 percent of Thompson's fourth grade students scored at or above proficiency level (proficient or advanced) on the CSAP reading test; in 1999, 73 percent scored at or above proficiency—an increase in performance that yielded the third highest learning growth rank among Colorado's 176 school districts. Similarly, in 1997, 35 percent of Thompson's fourth graders passed the CSAP writing assessment at or above the proficient level, and in 1999, 49 percent scored proficient or higher. This increase in performance on the fourth grade writing assessment was the highest in Colorado. Comparably impressive results were achieved by Thompson's seventh graders across the same three-year period, 1997-1999.

Another reflection of the teacher evaluation system's impact on school improvement relates to how teachers are changing and improving their instruction. School-wide performance assessment is linked closely to instructional improvement activities. In Thompson's standards-based system, a behaviorally anchored scoring rubric is used to assess how well a school's improvement plan relates to student achievement. Then, based on actual student performance in a given school, recommendations are made for next steps in school improvement planning, including teacher professional development. This process allows teachers "to define the next steps they need in training and, in essence, individualizes and pinpoints needed staff development."[196] As an example of how this systematic focus on student learning is affecting instruction, a 1999 survey of the district's teachers revealed that 94 percent used both formal and informal assessments to track student progress on standards and 93 percent used results of student assessments to alter instruction for individual students or the class. The school superintendent summarized improvements in both student learning gains and in teacher performance as follows: "This district has shown the ability to improve student performance on state assessments more than most districts. [Additionally] there is a focus on teacher behaviors that promote student achievement. That's paying off."[197]

In addition to the hard evidence of rising student achievement scores, there appears to be a peripheral benefit of a heightened awareness throughout the district of the importance of student results. Randy Zila, director of human resources, who was a chief architect involved in assessing the results of the evaluation system, summed up this attitude: "Student achievement has been on the rise; we continue to show growth. Students in their own language are talking about standards. They know what is expected of them and what they should be able to do."[198] Responding from a classroom perspective, one elementary teacher summarized the impact of the teacher-student assessment system on her students thus: "I'm more aware of how my students are achieving. I have data, now, to show parents how their children are learning. It is based more on hard data and not on feelings. It's not just instinct—it's *provable*."[199]

Conclusion

As with any teacher evaluation system, there are distinctive advantages and disadvantages embedded in Thompson's standards-based approach. There are numerous aspects of the Thompson School District standards and evaluation system in need of continued work and improvement; nonetheless, there are many aspects of this effort that may be well worth replicating. Although there were caveats in their comments, teachers who had participated in Thompson's standards-based teacher evaluation system were quite positive. The following comments reflect a summary of the perspectives they offered:

- "I would go with it absolutely—*if* based on student growth. That is what our job is—to teach children, and teaching means students should learn. [However], can you measure every part of student learning—no. Teachers need to make every effort for student growth to occur, but other factors have to be accounted for."[200]
- "Yes. I absolutely believe we should be held accountable. If students aren't learning, we should be able to document what we have done to encourage their learning."[201]

Beyond the technical-rational aspects of the evaluation system that other school districts might want to consider, both the school superintendent and one of the teachers interviewed offered nearly identical advice regarding the importance of the change process that bears repeating: "To bring this change, there must be a collaborative partnership between teachers and administrators." "There must be trust." Thus, an important lesson to be learned here is that not only is the final *product*—the teacher evaluation system—important, but also the *process* used to develop, implement, and support this important change must be carefully and thoughtfully constructed.

VII.

TEACHER EVALUATION AND STUDENT ACHIEVEMENT: WHAT ARE THE LESSONS LEARNED AND WHERE DO WE GO FROM HERE?

What are the lessons learned about using student achievement in teacher evaluation? Through the review of research as well as drawing from the four case studies presented in the previous chapters, we have attempted to illuminate issues related to the relationship between student learning and teacher evaluation. We have examined and critiqued a range of possible strategies that measure student learning and link it to teacher evaluation. In this final chapter, we briefly examine lessons learned from using student assessment in teacher evaluation, including potential benefits and liabilities. Then, we offer a set of recommendations to guide the application of student assessment to teacher evaluation.

What Are the Lessons Learned About Using Student Assessment in Teacher Evaluation?

In Dallas and Tennessee, where gain scores on standardized achievement tests have been used, there have been increases in student achievement levels. Test results have been used in both systems to inform teacher evaluation and to guide improvement assistance. In Dallas, test results are integrated into the instructional improvement plan developed by each teacher. In Tennessee, test results are used as one data point, along with more clinical approaches, in evaluation. In Oregon and the Thompson, Colorado, School District, where the impact of teacher performance on student learning has been documented with more of a mixed design (qualitative and quantitative measures), the promise and evidence for focused teacher efforts and improved student learning also exist. In the Oregon Work Sample Methodology, actual samples of teacher work are assessed for their connection to classroom-based student learning. In the Thompson, Colorado, School District, teacher job performance standards are connected directly to student learning, using both class-

Table 3

What Are the Implications for Using Student Assessment in Teacher Evaluation?

Implications	Dallas: Comparative Student Growth Model	Tennessee: Repeated Measures of Student Gain Model	Oregon: Work Sample Methodology Model	Thompson School District (CO): Standards Based Model
Student learning	There has been a general trend of increasing student scores on the norm-referenced ITBS and the criterion-referenced, state test, TAAS.[202]	Increased student achievement has been documented in math, science, and language with reading and social studies remaining relatively constant.	The TWSM is an authentic and applied appraisal system that is designed to portray student learning progress as "outcomes desired by a teacher and taught by a teacher."	The system is designed to increase "the probability of advancing student learning." As measured by various standardized achievement tests, student learning has improved.
Instructional assistance for students	Assistance is provided in evaluating student abilities and responding to needs with classroom regrouping, tutoring, and summer school.	Emphasis has been on teaching the curriculum more thoroughly with built-in review. Students are regrouped more frequently to focus instruction on weaker skills or concepts.	Because of the "action research" nature of the TWSM, a key benefit is early and direct classroom instructional assistance for individual students and students clustered by learning needs.	The system encourages teachers to focus on individual student learning needs through content standards, learning styles, teaching/learning strategies, and assessment of learning results.
Personnel actions	Test results are integrated into the Instructional Improvement Plan for each teacher. They are used for remediation when needed.	Test results are one source of data but cannot be the sole source of information for evaluation. They are used for remediation when needed.	The Oregon TWSM, to date, has been used in initial teacher licensure. It has proven to be a viable tool for screening candidates for entry into the teaching profession.	Teacher performance standards are clearly delineated, assessed partially on student learning, and then tied to professional development. The focus of the system is on performance assistance and improvement.
Professional development	Professional development needs, as reflected in summative teacher evaluations, are left to the discretion of the local school.	Focused professional development on implementation of TAAS objectives and specific skill development for teachers.	The TWSM is designed to foster both formative and summative teacher reflection and self-evaluation.	The results of the evaluation cycle for each teacher are connected to professional development needs in the upcoming evaluation cycle.

room indices and standardized tests as measures of student learning. A summary of key features from the four teacher evaluation systems is provided in Table 3.

In all four of the case studies presented in this book, test data are used as one of multiple measures of teacher effectiveness. Student achievement results have been used to focus professional development, often on issues of practice and what works to enhance learning for children. Teachers who have been more successful in achieving high student performance have been identified and encouraged to share their instructional strategies. Moreover, in each of these teacher evaluation systems the application of student learning to teacher evaluation is designed to foster both formative and summative teacher evaluation and, ultimately, increased student learning.

Student assessment measures are a source of information that can be used to simply sort and rank based on a set of criteria or to diagnostically enhance instruction and services at the individual, school, or program level. If thoughtfully used, they can "guide investments in school and teacher learning linked to changes in practice" as suggested by Linda Darling-Hammond.[203] In response to better identified shortcomings in the current use of resources, schools are beginning to experiment with regrouping, more structured diagnostic assessments, different uses of time for different children, and better articulation of the curriculum. The use of student assessment information can inform research on the impact of these reform efforts, to confirm anecdotal reports of success and explore the unintended consequences as well.

When linking student learning with teacher effectiveness, it is important to remember that tests and other types of student assessments are objective entities and have the potential for benefit or misuse. Nonetheless, educators should embrace the possibilities of using student achievement measures as a tool, one of many, to make education more meaningful and productive for students of all ability levels.

What Are the Basic Requirements of Fair Testing Programs That Are To Be Used To Inform Teacher Evaluation?

When student learning measures are used in the evaluation of teachers and other educators, they must conform to professional standards of practice.[204] Certainly there are numerous challenges and potential pitfalls to the unschooled use of assessment data for evaluation of any sort, particularly for use in personnel evaluation; therefore, it is important to maximize the benefits and minimize the liabilities in the connection of student learning and teacher effectiveness. Thus, we propose the following practices to reduce possible bias and increase fairness when using student assessment data to evaluate educational personnel:

1. Use student learning as only one component of a teacher evaluation system that is based on multiple data sources.

We maintain that measures of student learning are vitally important to judging the effectiveness of teachers and schools, but they should never serve as the sole source for evaluating performance. Rather, multiple sources of information should be considered in order that a more complete picture of performance can be developed. Such multiple data sources might include formal and informal observations, client surveys, artifacts of performance, goal setting, and other relevant sources of performance information. Student learning measures should be considered in conjunction with these other sources.

Single indicators of student learning should not usurp professional judgment that integrates knowledge of other factors that affect instruction, like lack of resources, overcrowding, and community poverty. Teaching and learning is far too complex a phenomenon to be reduced to a single test result. Tests, however, can serve as gauges of other problems in specific classrooms or schools that need to be addressed through staff development, teacher mentoring, greater resources, or reorganization of time and curriculum.

As discussed in chapter II, the use of test results in teacher evaluation can be considered as a viable complement to traditional supervision based on classroom observations and other pertinent data sources. Supervision provides information on the *means* of teaching, the decisions that are made in the selection, organization, and delivery of instruction. Test results provide information on the *ends* of teaching. Evaluation of the means seems meaningless without some gauge of the ends. But on the other hand, the ends can never justify questionable means. A balanced approach to evaluation would consider both by using multiple measures.

2. When judging teacher effectiveness, consider the context in which teaching and learning occur.

The Tennessee Value-Added Assessment System studies reported that "the two most important factors impacting student gain are the teacher and the achievement level for the student"[205] [i.e., how much students had achieved prior to coming to a given classroom]. Moreover, the studies provided evidence that teacher effectiveness is a far more powerful determinant of student learning than selected contextual variables. The researchers concluded that:

> Differences in teacher effectiveness were found to be the dominant factor affecting student academic gain. The importance of the effects of certain classroom contextual variables (class size and classroom heterogeneity) appears to be minor . . .[206]

Despite these impressive findings, we contend that there are occasions when teachers have done everything possible at the classroom level to enhance instruction but conditions beyond their control, such as unreasonably large class sizes or classes taught in the cafeteria, prevent maximum benefit to children. Thus, we recommend that consideration be given for student mobility, absenteeism, and other variables beyond the control of the teacher. The whole system of support, including staff training, availability of mentors, and workspaces, books, and instructional materials that are conducive to learning cannot be overlooked in attributing responsibility for learning. Until teachers teach in fully supportive environments, these circumstances must be taken into account.

3. Use measures of student growth versus a fixed achievement standard or goal.

In the world beyond schools, very few human endeavors are judged in terms of fixed goals; more typically, they are based on growth and progress toward stated goals. Even the hard-nosed world of business judges performance based on a variety of economic indicators and comparisons to projected growth. We propose that the same paradigm be used in education with an acknowledgment of possible learning inhibitors and comparisons to projected learning growth. This approach requires the use of pre- and post-testing to determine progress versus the attainment of predetermined pass rates or proficiency levels. While there is a place and purpose for fixed standards, such as learning to read at an acceptable level, fixed standards must be regarded skeptically when applied to personnel evaluation.

When student learning is communicated in terms of absolute achievement (e.g., 70 percent correct on Reading Comprehension), it perpetuates a meritocracy of the "haves" and the "have nots." As observed by James Popham,[207] absolute achievement scores tend to reflect what children bring to school and not necessarily what they have learned in school. Absolute achievement scores also tend to preserve the notion that it is aptitude that counts in school and not effort. Not only is this a counterproductive idea for students of all ability levels, but also it runs directly counter to a standard of fairness in teacher evaluation. If student learning is truly our goal in schools, we must create environments for effort-based learning as described by Lauren Resnick[208] with the focus on achievement growth. True measures of learning should focus on growth in knowledge and skills, not on student aptitude.

The use of absolute achievement scores also penalizes the teachers who and schools that work with the least prepared and most challenging learners. When you begin with a high achieving group, "good" test results are a foregone conclusion and vice versa. What is the incentive for students, teachers, or schools to invest a great deal of effort in learning when the goal is almost always out of reach? Our most effective teachers are those who take all students from where they are academically and creatively respond to their learning needs and interests. Effective teachers move students forward and assist them in achieving definable academic goals.

4. Compare learning gains from one point in time to another for the same students, not different groups of students.

Implicit in the concept of gain scores is the assumption that similar tests will be used to measure student learning across time on an individual basis. When student learning is aggregated across a class of students, a reasonably fair measure of teacher effects is generated. Teacher effects are not gauged in a fair manner, however, when the absolute achievement level of one class of students is compared to the absolute achievement of a different class of students. While this is common practice at the school and school district level, it is unfair and unreasonable at the individual teacher level. It holds teachers accountable for the performance of two different groups of students with potentially discrepant sets of prerequisite knowledge and skills. This type of comparison invites a bias in measuring gain scores that should be eliminated, not perpetuated.

5. Recognize that gain scores have pitfalls that must be avoided.

Even when measures of student growth are used, it is critical to properly interpret gain scores. In particular, a statistical artifact known as the regression effect needs to be considered. It results in a tendency for students starting with low performance levels to show larger gains than warranted. Conversely, students who start with high performance may show lower gains, or even declines, if the measure of student achievement is not adequately difficult to gauge what those high-scoring students know.[209]

6. Use a time frame for teacher evaluation that allows for patterns of student learning to be documented.

If teachers are to be held accountable for student learning, then it is critical that patterns of student learning be established—not single snapshots. We support the suggestion by Sanders and his colleagues "that teacher evaluation processes should include, as a major component, a reliable and valid measure of a teacher's effect on student academic growth over time."[210]

Repeated measures of student learning over time enhance reliability from a statistical point of view and credibility from a decision-making perspective. The scoring errors made by CTB/McGraw-Hill in 1998-99 emphasize the serious consequences of placing too much credence on a single set of test results.[211] The test results for students in six states were compromised by the errors and over 8,000 students in New York City alone were required to attend summer school based on low test scores that were incorrect. In contrast, Tennessee, which had longitudinal data on most of its students, was able to flag the errors in the testing reports before they were distributed to schools and students.[212] They delayed critical decision-making until they had corrected test results, thus demonstrating the power of using repeated measures of student learning.

7. Use fair and valid measures of student learning.

Reliability, validity, freedom from bias, and fairness are obvious concerns and conditions for connecting student assessment to teacher evaluation. Drawing on the work of Wheeler,[213] McConney, Schalock, and Schalock,[214] and others,[215] we propose several practices to increase the fairness of using student assessment data to evaluate educational personnel. Specifically, the use of student assessment measures in evaluating teacher performance should be:

- *Valid.* "Any measure of student performance, whether used for formative or summative evaluation, should be sensitive to (be able to detect) the impacts of what teachers and schools do; that is, measures of student learning should have instructional validity. If they do not…then it would be hard to justify their use for either teacher or school evaluation of any kind."[216]

- *Reliable.* The assessment measure should produce adequately consistent (i.e., reliable) results across time and across scorers.[217]
- *Free from bias.* Student achievement data should be used in an objective, fair, and impartial manner, and should not be interpreted or used capriciously.
- *Comparable.* Results for one teacher should be comparable to results for other teachers. "No teacher...should be disadvantaged compared with any other based on factors beyond their control."[218]

8. Select student assessment measures that are most closely aligned with existing curriculum.

Given that there are no national curriculum standards, test makers must make choices in what content they select for inclusion on standardized tests and other measures of student performance. Their selections may or may not reflect state or local curriculum. Some states have contracted for the development of customized tests that reflect the state mandated curriculum but even then there can be incongruities with delivery of the curriculum in different school districts, schools, and classrooms. Standardized tests will never be perfectly aligned with delivered curriculum; only the classroom teacher can ensure that level of alignment, which supports the need for a variety of assessment strategies. Standardized tests, however, should be selected based on their general or predominant alignment with the articulated curriculum.

When standardized measures of student achievement are selected without regard to the curriculum, they do not fairly reflect teaching or learning except in a very general sense. They may reflect a general body of knowledge and skills acquired in school or at home, but they do not reflect specific instruction by a particular teacher during a precise period of time. If student assessment measures are unrelated to what has been taught, then they cannot be used to measure the impact of teaching.

> Any measure of student performance, whether used for formative or summative teacher or school evaluation, should be consistent with the curricula of courses, programs, and/or schools. The measures should reflect both the scope and complexity of the content taught. If they do not, then it would be hard to defend the claim that a full and representative sample of teachers' or schools' work is reflected by student performance data. Worse, it may be that the student performance measures assess content that is not part of the curricula of courses, programs, and/or schools. This would be akin to holding teachers and schools accountable for outcomes for which they are not responsible.[219]

Tests that are disconnected from curriculum may provide a gauge of what students know compared to other students in the same grade across the nation, but they hardly provide a basis for judging teaching effectiveness. The value of student assessment measures for educators is proportional to their alignment with the curriculum. Thus, student achievement measures used in teacher evaluation must have sufficient curriculum validity.

9. Do not narrow the curriculum and limit teaching to fit a test.

Another unintended but predictable consequence of selecting standardized tests that are not aligned with the curriculum is the distortion of the curriculum to meet the demands of the test. A basic educational principle is the alignment of curriculum, instruction, and assessment. Ideally, curriculum and instruction drive assessment, but if assessment is fixed and determines high stakes decisions such as teacher evaluation, then it can drive the curriculum and instruction. This is a subversion of the educational process by allowing tests and test makers to determine the content and pacing of teaching. No one intends for this to happen, but evidence abounds that it is occurring, and it is one of the reasons many teachers object to testing programs. This concern seems justified based on a standard of fairness.

A Final Note

If there is any lesson to be learned from these chapters, it is that teachers make a difference in student learning. Given the clear and undeniable link that exists between teacher effectiveness and student learning, can be, indeed should be, an important source of feedback on the effectiveness of schools, administrators, and teachers. However, student achievement should be used in conjunction with other evidence of teacher performance and productivity, and never in isolation. The challenge for educators and policy makers is to make certain that student achievement is placed in the broader context of multiple indicators of what teachers are accomplishing. Nonetheless, we think the conclusion is self-evident: student learning is connected to teacher performance and, thus, measures of teacher performance—teacher evaluation—can be connected to student learning.

NOTES

[1] See Cawelti, G. (1999). Improving achievement: Finding research-based practices and programs that boost student achievement. *The American School Board Journal,* 186 (7), 34-37. Also, see Finn, J. D., & Achilles, C. M. (1999). Tennessee's class size study: Findings, implications, misconceptions. *Educational Evaluation and Policy Analysis,* 21, 97-110.

[2] Traina, R. P. (1999, January 20). What makes a good teacher? *Education Week, 18,* 34.

[3] Johnston, R. C. (1999, May 12). Texas study links teacher certification, student success *Education Week, 18,* 19-20.

[4] John Cole, President, Texas Federation of Teachers. Cited in Johnston, 1999, p. 20.

[5] The Tennessee Value-Added Research and Assessment Center work will be highlighted in more detail in Chapter 4.

[6] Taken from presentation made by William Sanders at the College of William and Mary School Leadership Institute, Williamsburg, Va., June 29, 1999.

[7] Wright, S. P., Horn, S. P., & Sanders, W. L. (1997). Teacher and classroom context effects on student achievement: Implications for teacher evaluation. *Journal of Personnel Evaluation in Education,* 11, 57-67, p. 63.

[8] Sanders, W. L., & Rivers, J. C. (1996). *Cumulative and residual effects of teachers on future student academic achievement* (Research Progress Report). Knoxville, Tenn.: University of Tennessee Value-Added Research and Assessment Center.

[9] Sanders, W. L., & Rivers, J. C., 1996, p. 63.

[10] Wright, Horn, & Sanders, 1997, p. 57.

[11] Mendro, R. L. (1998). Student achievement and school and teacher accountability. *Journal of Personnel Evaluation in Education,* 12, 257-267, p. 262. The Dallas Public Schools program will be highlighted in more detail in chapter 3.

[12] Mendro, 1998, p. 261.

[13] See 1) Sanders & Rivers, 1996. 2) Jordan, H., Mendro, R., & Weerasinghe, D. (1997, July). *Teacher effects on longitudinal student achievement.* Paper presented at the Sixth Annual Evaluation Institute sponsored by CREATE, Indianapolis, IN. 3) Bembry, K., Jordan, H., Gomez, E., Anderson, M., & Mendro, R. (1998, April). *Policy implications of long-term teacher effects on student achievement.* Paper presented at the annual meeting of the American Educational Research Association, San Diego, Calif.

[14] Mendro, 1998, p. 261.

[15] Chase, B. (1999, February 28). Show me the data! In education reform, the age of accountability has arrived (Paid advertisement). *The Washington Post,* p. B2.

[16] Mobil Corporation. (1999, February 28). Are schools improving? Too many educated guesses (Paid advertisement). *The Washington Post,* p. B24.

[17] Broder, D. (1999, February 28). No magic for the schools. *The Washington Post,* p. B7.

[18] McConney, A. A., Schalock, M. D., & Schalock, H. D. (1997). Indicators of student learning in teacher evaluation. In J. H. Stronge (Ed.), *Evaluating teaching: A guide to current thinking and best practice* (pp. 162-192). Thousand Oaks, Calif.: Corwin Press, p. 162.

[19] National Commission on Teaching and America's Future. (1996). *What matters most: Teaching for America's future.* New York: Author.

[20] National Commission on Teaching and America's Future, 1996, p. 18.

[21] Although there are good examples of school-based performance assessment systems, we chose to exclude those from this study and, rather, to concentrate on approaches that focus on individual teacher performance and student learning.

[22] Eisner, E. W. (1999). The uses and limits of performance assessment. *Phi Delta Kappan, 80,* 658-661, p. 658.

[23] Brophy, J., & Good, T. (1986). Teacher behavior and student achievement. In M.C. Wittrock (Ed.), *Handbook of research on teaching* (3rd ed., pp. 329-375). New York: Macmillan.

[24] Alkin, M. C. (1992). *Encyclopedia of educational research, volume 4* (6th ed.). New York: Macmillan, p. 1375.

[25] Brophy, J., & Good, T. L. (1986), p. 328.

[26] Roy Kemble, personal communication, May 24, 1999.

[27] Hoff, D. J. (1999, June 16). Made to measure. *Education Week, 18,* 21-27.

[28] Hoff, 1999.

[29] Olson, L. (1998, December 16). Quality counts '99 to track accountability in states. *Education Week, 18,* 10.

[30] Salvia, J., & Ysseldyke, J. E. (1998). *Assessment* (7th ed.). Boston: Houghton Mifflin, p. 432.

[31] Eisner, 1999, p. 659.

[32] Schalock, H. D., & Schalock, M. D. (1993). Student learning in teacher evaluation and school improvement: An introduction. *Journal of Personnel Evaluation in Education, 7,* 103-104, p. 103.

[33] Schalock & Schalock, 1993, p. 103.

[34] See Wright, S. P., Horn, S. P., & Sanders, W. L. (1997). Teacher and classroom context effects on student achievement: Implications for teacher evaluation. *Journal of Personnel Evaluation in Education, 11,* 57-67. Also see Bembry, K., Jordan, H., Gomez, E., Anderson, M., & Mendro, R. (1998, April). *Policy implications of long-term teacher effects on student achievement.* Paper presented at the annual meeting of the American Educational Research Association, San Diego, Calif.

[35] Thum, Y. M., & Bryk, A. S. (1997). Value-added productivity indicators: The Dallas system. In J. Millman (Ed.), *Grading teachers, grading schools: Is student achievement a valid evaluation measure?* (pp. 100-109). Thousand Oaks, Calif.: Corwin Press.

[36] Webster, W. J., & Mendro, R. L. (1997). The Dallas value-added accountability system. In J. Millman (Ed.), *Grading teachers, grading schools: Is student achievement a valid evaluation measure?* (pp. 81-99). Thousand Oaks, Calif.: Corwin Press.

[37] Dallas Public Schools. (1998). *Teacher appraisal system manual.* Dallas, Tex.: Author, p. 2.

[38] Webster & Mendro, 1997, p. 82.

[39] Dallas Public Schools. (1997). *School performance improvement awards 1997-98.* Dallas, Tex.: Author, p. 11.

[40] Dallas Public Schools, 1997.

[41] Webster & Mendro, 1997, p. 81.

[42] Mendro, R. L. (1998). Student achievement and school and teacher accountability. *Journal of Personnel Evaluation in Education, 12,* 257-267, p. 261.

[43] Webster & Mendro, 1997, p. 83.

[44] Dallas Public Schools, 1997, p. 12.

[45] Webster & Mendro, 1997.

[46] Dallas Public Schools, 1997.

[47] Bearden, D. K., Bembry, K. L., & Babu, S. (1995, April). *Effective schools: Is there a win-*

ning combination of administrators, teachers, and students? Paper presented at the annual meeting of the American Educational Research Association, San Francisco, Calif.

[48] Webster & Mendro, 1997.

[49] Webster & Mendro, 1997, p. 90.

[50] Dallas Public Schools, 1998, p. 18.

[51] Webster & Mendro, 1997, p. 85. Also, see Webster & Mendro for a more detailed explanation of the calculations and a rationale for the statistical approach used in the assessment system.

[52] Dallas Public Schools, 1997, p. 11.

[53] Dallas Public Schools, 1997, p. 4.

[54] There are 12 schools that are not yet included in the accountability process due to fairness issues that are raised by the nature of the school or the student enrollment.

[55] Dallas Public Schools, 1998, p. 2.

[56] Webster, W. J., Mendro, R. L., Orsak, T., Weerasinghe, D., & Bembry, K. (1997). Little practical difference and pie in the sky: A response to Thum and Bryk and a rejoinder to Sykes. In J. Millman (Ed.), *Grading teachers, grading schools: Is student achievement a valid evaluation measure?* (pp. 120-130). Thousand Oaks, Calif.: Corwin Press, p. 129.

[57] Mendro, 1998, p. 263.

[58] Bembry, K. (1999, July). *Developing joint ownership within a teacher appraisal system.* Paper presented at the annual National Evaluation Institute, Traverse City, Mich.

[59] Cunningham, L. L. (1997). In the beginning. In J. Millman (Ed.), *Grading teachers, grading schools: Is student achievement a valid evaluation measure?* Thousand Oaks, Calif.: Corwin Press, p. 76.

[60] Sykes, G. (1997). On trial: The Dallas value-added accountability system. In J. Millman (Ed.), *Grading teachers, grading schools: Is student achievement a valid evaluation measure?* (pp. 110-119). Thousand Oaks, Calif.: Corwin Press, pp. 111-112.

[61] Darling-Hammond, L. (1997). Toward what end? The evaluation of student learning for the improvement of teaching. In J. Millman (Ed.), *Grading teachers, grading schools: Is student achievement a valid evaluation measure?* (pp. 248-263). Thousand Oaks, Calif.: Corwin Press.

[62] Thum and Bryk, 1997.

[63] Roy Kemble, personal communication, May 24, 1999.

[64] Mendro, 1998.

[65] Tracie Fraley, personal communication, May 24, 1999; Linda Brackenridge, personal communication, May 25, 1999.

[66] Education Improvement Act, 9 Ten. Stat. Ann. §§49-1-603-608 (1990 Supp. 1992).

[67] Sanders, W. L., & Horn, S. P. (1994). The Tennessee Value-Added Assessment System (TVAAS): Mixed-model methodology in educational assessment. *Journal of Personnel Evaluation in Education, 8,* 299-311, p. 301.

[68] Ceperley, P. E., & Reel, K. (1997). The impetus for the Tennessee Value-Added Accountability System. In J. Millman (Ed.), *Grading teachers, grading schools: Is student achievement a valid evaluation measure?* (pp. 133-136). Thousand Oaks, Calif.: Corwin Press, pp. 135-136.

[69] Ceperley & Reel, 1997.

[70] Sanders, W. L., Saxton, A. M., & Horn, S. P. (1997). The Tennessee Value-Added Accountability System: A quantitative, outcomes-based approach to educational assessment. In J. Millman (Ed.), *Grading teachers, grading schools: Is student achievement a valid evaluation measure?* (pp. 137-162). Thousand Oaks, Calif.: Corwin Press, p. 141.

[71] Until 1999, the CTBS/4 constituted the norm-referenced portion of the test used by TVAAS. In 1999, Tennessee switched to TerraNova.

[72] TerraNova is a relatively new test developed by McGraw/Hill.

[73] University of Tennessee Value-Added Research and Assessment Center. (1997). *Graphical summary of educational findings from the Tennessee Value-Added Assessment System.* Knoxville, Tenn.: Author.

[74] Sanders, Saxton, & Horn, 1997, p. 139.

[75] Sanders, W. L., & Horn, S. P. (1998). Research findings from the Tennessee Value-Added Assessment System (TVAAS) database: Implications for education evaluation and research. *Journal of Personnel Evaluation in Education, 12,* 247-256, p. 251.

[76] Darlington, R. B. (1997). The Tennessee Value-Added Assessment System: A challenge to familiar assessment methods. In J. Millman (Ed.), *Grading teachers, grading schools: Is student achievement a valid evaluation measure?* (pp. 163-168). Thousand Oaks, Calif.: Corwin Press.

[77] Wright, S. P., Horn, S. P., & Sanders, W. L. (1997). Teacher and classroom context effects on student achievement: Implications for teacher evaluation. *Journal of Personnel Evaluation in Education, 11,* 57-67.

[78] Wright, Horn, & Sanders, 1997.

[79] Sanders, Saxton, & Horn, 1997.

[80] Sanders, Saxton, & Horn, 1997, p. 143.

[81] Sanders & Horn, 1998, p. 255.

[82] Sanders & Horn, 1994, p. 303.

[83] Sanders, W. L., & Horn, S. P. (1995). *An overview of the Tennessee Value-Added Assessment System.* Knoxville, Tenn.: University of Tennessee Value-Added Research and Assessment Center.

[84] Sanders, Saxton, & Horn, 1997, p. 181.

[85] Walberg, H. J., & Paik, S. J. (1997). Assessment requires incentives to add value: A review of the Tennessee value-added assessment system. In J. Millman (Ed.), *Grading teachers, grading schools: Is student achievement a valid evaluation measure?* (pp. 169-178). Thousand Oaks, Calif.: Corwin Press.

[86] Walberg & Paik, 1997, p. 171.

[87] Teachers at Carter Elementary School, personal communication, June 4, 1999.

[88] Glenda Russell, math teacher, personal communication, June 8, 1999.

[89] Bratton, S. E., Jr., Horn, S. P., & Wright, S. P. (1996). *Using and interpreting Tennessee's Value-Added Assessment System: A primer for teachers and principals.* [Booklet]. Knoxville, Tenn.: University of Tennessee.

[90] Bratton, Horn, & Wright, 1996, p. 26-28.

[91] Teachers at Carter Elementary School, personal communication, June 4, 1999.

[92] McLean, R. A., & Sanders. W. L. (1984). *Objective component of teacher evaluation: A feasibility study* (Working Paper No. 199). Knoxville, Tenn.: University of Tennessee, College of Business Administration.

[93] Sanders, Saxton, & Horn, 1997, p. 161.

[94] Gary Harman, President of the Knox County Education Association, personal communication, June 4, 1999.

[95] Gary Harman, President of the Knox County Education Association, personal communication, June 4, 1999.

[96] Bratton, Horn, & Wright, 1996, p. 30.

[97] Darling-Hammond, L. (1997). Toward what end? The evaluation of student learning for the improvement of teaching. In J. Millman (Ed.), *Grading teachers, grading schools: Is student achievement a valid evaluation measure?* (pp. 248-263). Thousand Oaks, Calif.: Corwin Press, p. 250.

[98] University of Tennessee Value-Added Research and Assessment Center, 1997.

[99] University of Tennessee Value-Added Research and Assessment Center, 1997.

[100] Glenda Russell, math teacher, personal communication, June 8, 1999.

[101] Glenda Russell, math teacher, personal communication, June 8, 1999.

[102] Archer, J. (1999, May 5). Sanders 101. *Education Week, 18,* 27.

[103] Rick Privette, Principal at Carter Elementary School in Knox County, personal communication, June 4, 1999.

[104] Sanders, Saxton, & Horn, 1997.

[105] Sanders & Horn, 1994, p. 301.

[106] Del Schalock, Teaching Research Division, Western Oregon University, personal communication, June 11, 1999.

[107] Airasian, P. W. (1997). Oregon Teacher Work Sample Methodology: Potential and problems. In J. Millman (Ed.), *Grading teachers, grading schools: Is student achievement a valid evaluation measure?* (pp. 46-52). Thousand Oaks, Calif.: Corwin Press, p. 47.

[108] Del Schalock, personal communication, June 11, 1999.

[109] McConney, A. A., Schalock, M. D., & Schalock, H. D. (1998). Focusing improvement and quality assurance: Work samples as authentic performance measures of prospective teachers' effectiveness. *Journal of Personnel Evaluation in Education, 11,* 343-363, p. 345.

[110] McConney, Schalock, & Schalock, 1998, p. 345.

[111] Wolf, K., Lichtenstein, G., & Stevenson, C. (1997). Portfolios in teacher evaluation. In J. H. Stronge (Ed.), *Evaluating teaching: A guide to current thinking and best practice* (pp. 193-214). Thousand Oaks, Calif.: Corwin Press, p. 193.

[112] McConney, A. A., Schalock, M. D., & Schalock, H. D. (1997). Indicators of student learning in teacher evaluation. In J. H. Stronge (Ed.), *Evaluating teaching: A guide to current thinking and best practice* (pp. 162-192). Thousand Oaks, Calif.: Corwin Press, p. 173.

[113] McConney, Schalock, & Schalock, 1997, p. 172.

[114] Western Oregon University. (No date). *Teacher Effectiveness Project - The reliability and validity of Teacher Work Sample Methodology: A synopsis.* Monmouth, Ore.: Author, p. 1.

[115] Western Oregon University, no date, p. 9.

[116] Western Oregon University, no date, pp. 10-11.

[117] Scriven, M. (1994). Duties of the teacher. *Journal of Personnel Evaluation in Education, 8,* 151-184.

[118] Danielson, C. (1996). *Enhancing professional practice: A framework for teaching.* Alexandria, Va.: Association for Supervision and Curriculum Development.

[119] National Board for Professional Teaching Standards. (1989). *Toward high and rigorous standards for the teaching profession.* Washington, D.C.: Author.

[120] While appropriate for the intended purpose of comparing the TWSM with Oregon's teacher licensure requirements, this definition of construct validity is narrower than would be desired for use of TWSM with evaluation of practicing teachers.

[121] Schalock, H. D., Schalock, M., & Girod, G. (1997). Teacher Work Sample Methodology as used at Western Oregon State University. In J. Millman (Ed.), *Grading teachers, grading schools: Is student achievement a valid evaluation measure?* (pp. 15-45). Thousand Oaks, Calif.: Corwin Press, p. 35.

[122] Western Oregon University, no date, p. 11.

[123] Millman, J. (1981). Student achievement as a measure of teaching competence. In J. Millman (Ed.), *Handbook of teacher evaluation* (pp. 146-166). Beverly Hills, Calif.: Sage.

[124] Schalock, Schalock, & Girod, 1997, pp. 22, 24-25.

[125] Cowart, B., & Myton, D. (1997). The Oregon Teacher Work Sample Methodology: Rationale and background. In J. Millman (Ed.), *Grading teachers, grading schools: Is student achievement a valid evaluation measure?* (pp. 11-14). Thousand Oaks, Calif.: Corwin Press, p. 18.

[126] Schalock, Schalock, & Girod, 1997, p. 18.

[127] Schalock, Schalock, & Girod, 1997, pp. 18-19.

[128] Western Oregon University, no date, p. 3.

[129] McConney, Schalock, & Schalock, 1997, p. 171.

[130] McConney, Schalock, & Schalock, 1997, p. 171.

[131] Our appreciation is extended to Rose Maxey for graciously allowing us to use a Work Sample she developed for a 3rd-4th grade combination class at Washington Elementary School, Salem-Keizer School District (Ore.), in this illustration.

[132] Western Oregon University, no date, p. 3.

[133] Western Oregon University, no date, p. 6.

[134] See Millman, J. (Ed.). (1997). *Grading teachers, grading schools: Is student achievement a valid evaluation measure?* Thousand Oaks, Calif.: Corwin Press.

[135] Schalock, Schalock, & Girod, 1997, p. 36.

[136] Susan Wood, Western Oregon University, personal communication, June 11, 1999.

[137] Stufflebeam, D. L. (1997). Oregon Teacher Work Sample Methodology: Educational policy review. In J. Millman (Ed.), *Grading teachers, grading schools: Is student achievement a valid evaluation measure?* (pp. 53-61). Thousand Oaks, Calif.: Corwin Press, p. 58.

[138] James Long, School of Education, Western Oregon University, personal communication, June 11, 1999.

[139] Sabrina Walker, teacher candidate, Western Oregon University, personal communication, June 11, 1999.

[140] Stufflebeam, 1997, p. 59.

[141] Del Schalock, Western Oregon University, personal communication, June 11, 1999.

[142] Susan Wood, Western Oregon University, personal communication, June 11, 1999.

[143] James Long, Western Oregon University, personal communication, June 11, 1999.

[144] Darling-Hammond, L. (1997). Toward what end? The evaluation of student learning for the improvement of teaching. In J. Millman (Ed.), *Grading teachers, grading schools: Is student achievement a valid evaluation measure?* (pp. 248-263). Thousand Oaks, Calif.: Corwin Press, p. 257.

[145] Airasian, 1997, p. 47.

[146] Robert Ayers, Teaching Research Division, Western Oregon University, personal communication, June 11, 1999.

[147] Rose Maxey, teacher candidate, Western Oregon University, personal communication, June 11, 1999.

[148] Airasian, 1997, pp. 49-50.

[149] Rose Maxey, Western Oregon University, personal communication, June 11, 1999.

[150] Rose Maxey, Western Oregon University, personal communication, June 11, 1999.

[151] Stufflebeam, 1997, p. 57.

[152] Stufflebeam, 1997, p. 58.

[153] Airasian, 1997, pp. 49-50.

[154] Sabrina Walker, Western Oregon University, personal communication, June 11, 1999.

[155] Stufflebeam, 1997, p. 60.

[156] Schalock, Schalock, & Girod, 1997, p. 38.

[157] Stufflebeam, 1997, p. 61.

[158] Darling-Hammond, 1997, p. 256.

[159] John Stewart, Assistant Superintendent, Thompson School District, personal communication, May 27, 1999.

[160] Thompson School District. (1996, August). *A parent's guide to standards.* Loveland, Colo.: Author.

[161] November, 1995

[162] Colorado House Bill 1338, House Bill 1159, and the Colorado Educator Licensing Act

[163] Thompson School District (No date). *School professional evaluation: Toolkit for administrators and school professionals.* Loveland, Colo.: Author, p. 1.

[164] Kuzmich, L., & Zila, R. (1998, December). *Developing standards-based professional goals as a focus for teacher evaluation.* Workshop presented at the National Staff Development Council, Washington, D.C.

[165] For a discussion of teacher evaluation based on job standards or duties, see: Scriven, M. (1988). Duties-based teacher evaluation. *Journal of Personnel Evaluation in Education, 1,* 319-334. Also see Stronge, J. H. (1997). Improving schools through teacher evaluation. In J. H. Stronge (Ed.), *Evaluating teaching: A guide to current thinking and best practice* (pp. 1-23). Thousand Oaks, Calif.: Corwin Press.

[166] Thompson School District. (1997-98). Teacher Professional Standards. *Thompson School District R2-J School Professional Evaluation Handbook.* Loveland, Colo.: Author, pp. 4-5.

[167] Thompson School District, 1997-98, p. 3.

[168] Don Saul, Superintendent of Schools, Thompson School District, personal communication, May 27, 1999.

[169] Kuzmich, L. (1998). *Data-driven instruction: A handbook for making decisions in standards-based classrooms.* rev. ed. Handout I-1. Longmont, Colo.: Centennial Board of Cooperative Services.

[170] Jim Neigherbauer, 6th grade teacher, Thompson School District, personal communication, May 27, 1999.

[171] Lin Kuzmich, elementary school principal, Thompson School District, personal communication, May 27, 1999.

[172] Don Saul, Thompson School District, personal communication, May 27, 1999.

[173] Randy Zila, Director of Human Resources, Thompson School District, personal communication, May 27, 1999.

[174] Jim Willard, Hewlett Packard executive and Thompson School Board member.

[175] Jim Neigherbauer, Thompson School District, personal communication, May 27, 1999.

[176] Nancy Popenhagen, Thompson Education Association (NEA) President, Thompson School District, personal communication, May 27, 1999.

[177] Lin Kuzmich, Thompson School District, personal communication, May 27, 1999.

[178] Randy Zila, Thompson School District, personal communication, May 27, 1999.

[179] Chris Love, 1st grade teacher, Thompson School District, personal communication, May 27, 1999.

[180] Jim Willard, Hewlett Packard executive and Thompson School Board member, personal communication, May 27, 1999.

[181] Randy Zila, Thompson School District, personal communication, May 27, 1999.

[182] Lin Kuzmich, Thompson School District, personal communication, May 27, 1999.

[183] Randy Zila, Thompson School District, personal communication, May 27, 1999.

[184] Don Saul, Thompson School District, personal communication, May 27, 1999.

[185] Chris Love, Thompson School District, personal communication, May 27, 1999.

[186] Don Saul, Thompson School District, personal communication, May 27, 1999.

[187] Jim Willard, Hewlett Packard executive and Thompson School Board member, personal communication, May 27, 1999.

[188] Nancy Popenhagen, Thompson School District, personal communication, May 27, 1999.

[189] Jim Neigherbauer, Thompson School District, personal communication, May 27, 1999.

[190] Chris Love, Thompson School District, personal communication, May 27, 1999.

[191] Nancy Popenhagen, Thompson School District, personal communication, May 27, 1999.

[192] Lin Kuzmich, Thompson School District, personal communication, May 27, 1999.

[193] Nancy Popenhagen, Thompson School District, personal communication, May 27, 1999.

[194] Lin Kuzmich, Thompson School District, personal communication, May 27, 1999.

[195] Jim Neigherbauer, Thompson School District, personal communication, May 27, 1999.

[196] Lin Kuzmich, Thompson School District, personal communication, October 22, 1999.

[197] Don Saul, Thompson School District, personal communication, May 27, 1999.

[198] Randy Zila, Thompson School District, personal communication, May 27, 1999.

[199] Chris Love, Thompson School District, personal communication, May 27, 1999.

[200] Nancy Popenhagen, Thompson School District, personal communication, May 27, 1999.

[201] Chris Love, Thompson School District, personal communication, May 27, 1999.

[202] Mendro, R. L. (1998). Student achievement and school and teacher accountability. *Journal of Personnel Evaluation in Education, 12*(3), 257-267.

[203] Darling-Hammond, L. (1997). *The right to learn: A blueprint for creating schools that work.* San Francisco: Jossey-Bass.

[204] See *The Personnel Evaluation Standards* (1988) by the Joint Committee on Standards for Educational Evaluation. Newbury Park, Calif.: Corwin Press.

[205] Wright, S. P., Horn, S. P., & Sanders, W. L. (1997). Teacher and classroom context effects on student achievement: Implications for teacher evaluation. *Journal of Personnel Evaluation in Education, 11,* 57–67, page 61.

[206] Wright, S. P., Horn, S. P., & Sanders, W. L. (1997), page 66.

[207] Popham, W. J. (1999). Why standardized tests don't measure educational quality. *Educational Leadership,* 56(6), 8-15.

[208] Resnick, L. B. (1999, June 16). Making America smarter. *Education Week, 18*(40), 38-40.

[209] Wheeler, P. H. (1996). Before you use student tests in teacher evaluation...consider these issues. *AASPA Report.* 3(3), 12-13. Virginia Beach, Va.: American Association of School Personnel Administrators.

[210] Wright, S. P., Horn, S. P., & Sanders, W. L. (1997), page 66.

[211] Viader, D., & Blair, J. (1999, September 29). Error affects test results in six states. Education Week, XIX(5), pp. 1, 13-15.

[212] Viader, D., & Blair, J. (1999).

[213] Wheeler, P. H. (1995). *AASPA Report.*

[214] McConney, A. A., Schalock, M. D., & Schalock, H. D. (1997). In J. H. Stronge (Ed.) *Evaluating teaching: A guide to current thinking and best practice* (pages 162-192). Thousand Oaks, Calif.: Corwin Press, Inc.

[215] See, for example, Haertel, E. (1986). The valid use of student performance measures for teacher evaluation. *Educational Evaluation and Policy Analysis, 8,* 45-60.

[216] McConney, A. A., Schalock, M. D., & Schalock, H. D. (1997), page 177. Curricular validity, a second aspect of validity that should be considered in settings such as proposed here, is discussed later in the chapter.

[217] Perfect consistency is rarely achieved, so an *acceptable level* of reliability, in measures such as inter-rater reliability, should be considered.

[218] McConney, A. A., Schalock, M. D., & Schalock, H. D. (1997), page 178.

[219] McConney, A. A., Schalock, M. D., & Schalock, H. D. (1997), page 177.

REFERENCES

Airasian, P.W. 1997. Oregon Teacher Work Sample Methodology: Potential and problems. In J. Millman (Ed.), *Grading teachers, grading schools: Is student achievement a valid evaluation measure?* Thousand Oaks, Calif.: Corwin Press.

Alkin, M.C. 1992. *Encyclopedia of educational research,* Volume 4 (6th ed.) New York: Macmillan.

Archer, J., Sanders. May 5, 1999. *Education Week* 18: 27.

Bearden, D.K., K.L. Bembry, and S. Babu. April 1995. *Effective schools: Is there a winning combination of administrators, teachers, and students?* Paper presented at the annual meeting of the American Educational Research Association, San Francisco, Calif.

Bembry, K. July 1999. *Developing joint ownership within a teacher appraisal system.* Paper presented at the annual National Evaluation Institute, Traverse City, Mich.

Bembry, K., H. Jordan, E. Gomez, M. Anderson, and R. Mendro. April 1998. *Policy implications of long-term teacher effects on student achievement.* Paper presented at the annual meeting of the American Educational Research Association, San Diego, Calif.

Bratton, S.E. Jr., S.P. Horn, and S.P. Wright. 1996. *Using and interpreting Tennessee's Value-Added Assessment System: A primer for teachers and principals.* [Booklet]. Knoxville, Tenn.: University of Tennessee.

Broder, D. February 28, 1999. No magic for the schools. *The Washington Post*: B7.

Brophy J., and T. Good. 1986. Teacher behavior and student achievement. In M.C. Wittrock (Ed.), *Handbook of research on teaching* (3rd ed.). New York: Macmillan: 329-275.

Cawelti, G., 1999. Improving achievement: Finding research-based practices and programs that boost student achievement. *The American School Board Journal,* 186(7): 34-37.

Ceperley, P.E., and K. Reel. 1997. The impetus for the Tennessee Value-Added Accountability System. In J. Millman (Ed.), *Grading teachers, grading schools: Is student achievement a valid evaluation measure?* Thousand Oaks, Calif.: Corwin Press.

Chase, B., February 28, 1999. Show me the data! In education reform, the age of accountability has arrived. (Paid advertisement.) *The Washington Post:* B2.

Cowart, B., and D. Myton. 1997. The Oregon Teacher Work Sample Methodology: Rationale and background. In J. Millman (Ed.), *Grading teachers, grading schools: Is student achievement a valid evaluation measure?* Thousand Oaks, Calif.: Corwin Press.

Cunningham, L.L. 1997. In the beginning. In J. Millman (Ed.), *Grading teachers, grading schools: Is student achievement a valid evaluation measure?* Thousand Oaks, Calif.: Corwin Press.

Dallas Public Schools. 1997. *School performance improvement awards 1997-98.* Dallas, Tex.: Author.

————. 1998. *Teacher appraisal system manual.* Dallas, Tex.: Author.

Danielson, C. 1996. *Enhancing professional practice: A framework for teaching.* Alexandria, Va.: Association for Supervision and Curriculum Development.

Darling-Hammond, L. 1997. *The right to learn: A blueprint for creating schools that work.* San Francisco: Jossey-Bass.

————. 1997. Toward what end? The evaluation of student learning for the improvement of teaching. In J. Millman (Ed.), *Grading teachers, grading schools: Is student achievement a valid evaluation measure?* Thousand Oaks, Calif.: Corwin Press.

Darlington, R.B. 1997. The Tennessee Value-Added Assessment System: A challenge to familiar assessment methods. In J. Millman (Ed.) *Grading teachers, grading schools: Is student achievement a valid evaluation measure?* Thousand Oaks, Calif.: Corwin Press.

Eisner, E.W. 1999. The uses and limits of performance assessment. *Phi Delta Kappan*, 80: 658-661.

Finn, J.D., and C.M. Achilles. 1999. Tennessee's class size study: Findings, implications, misconceptions. *Educational Evaluation and Policy Analysis* (21): 97-110.

Haertel, E. 1986. The valid use of student performance measures for teacher evaluation. *Educational Evaluation and Policy Analysis* (8): 45-60.

Hoff, D.J. June 16, 1999. Made to measure. *Education Week* 18: 21-27.

Johnston, R.C. May 12, 1999. Texas study links teacher certification, student success. *Education Week* 18: 19-20.

Joint Committee on Standards for Educational Evaluation. 1988. *The personnel evaluation standards*. Newbury Park, Calif.: Corwin Press.

Jordan, H., R. Mendro, and D. Weerasinghe, July 1997. Teacher effects on longitudinal student achievement. Paper presented at the Sixth Annual Evaluation Institute sponsored by CREATE, Indianapolis.

Kuzmich, L. 1998. *Data-driven instruction: A handbook for making decisions in standards-based classrooms*. rev. ed. Longmont, Colo.: Centennial Board of Cooperative Services. Cited in *Thompson School District School professional evaluation: Toolkit for administrators and school professionals*. Loveland, Colo.: Author.

Kuzmich, L., and R. Zila. December 1998. *Developing standards-based professional goals as a focus for teacher evaluation*. Workshop presented at the National Staff Development Council, Washington, D.C.

McConney, A.A., M.D. Schalock, and H.D. Schalock. 1997. Indicators of student learning in teacher evaluation. In J.H. Stronge (Ed.) *Evaluating teaching: A guide to current thinking and best practice*. Thousand Oaks, Calif.: Corwin Press.

———— . 1998. Focusing improvement and quality assurance: Work samples as authentic performance measures of prospective teachers' effectiveness. *Journal of Personnel Evaluation in Education* (11): 343-363.

McLean, R.A., and W.L. Sanders. 1984. *Objective component of teacher evaluation: A feasibility study* (Working Paper No. 199). Knoxville, Tenn.: University of Tennessee. College of Business Administration.

Mendro, R.L. 1998. Student achievement and school and teacher accountability. *Journal of Personnel Evaluation in Education,* 12(3): 257-267.

Millman, J. 1981. Student achievement as a measure of teaching competence. In J. Millman (Ed.), *Handbook of teacher evaluation*. Beverly Hills, Calif.: Sage.

Mobil Corporation. February 28, 1999. Are schools improving? Too many educated guesses. (Paid advertisement). *The Washington Post:* B24.

National Board for Professional Teaching Standards. 1989. *Toward high and rigorous standards for the teaching profession*. Washington, D.C.: Author.

National Commission on Teaching and America's Future. 1996. *What matters most: Teaching for America's future*. New York: Author.

Olson, L. December 16, 1998. Quality counts '99 to track accountability in states. *Education Week* 18: 10.

Popham, W.J. 1999. Why standardized tests don't measure educational quality. *Educational Leadership,* 56(6): 8-15.

Resnick, L.B. June 16, 1999. Making America smarter. *Education Week,* 18: 38-40.

Salvia, J., and J.E. Ysseldyke. 1998. *Assessment* (7th ed.). Boston: Houghton Mifflin.

Sanders, W.L., and S. P. Horn. 1994. The Tennessee Value-Added Assessment System (TVASS): Mixed-model methodology in educational assessment. *Journal of Personnel Evaluation in Education,* 8: 299-311.

———. 1995. *An overview of the Tennessee Value-Added Assessment System.* Knoxville, Tenn.: The University of Tennessee Value-Added Research and Assessment Center.

———. 1998. Research findings from the Tennessee Value-Added Assessment system (TVAAS) database: Implications for education evaluation and research. *Journal of Personnel Evaluation in Education,* 12: 247-256.

Sanders, W.L., and J. C. Rivers. 1996. *Cumulative and residual effects of teachers on future student academic achievement* (Research Progress Report). Knoxville, Tenn.: University of Tennessee Value-Added Reserch and Assessment Center.

Sanders, W.L., A.M. Saxton, and S.P. Horn. 1997. The Tennessee Value-Added Accountability System: A quantitative outcomes-based approach to educational assessment. In J. Millman (Ed.), *Grading teachers, grading schools: Is student achievement a valid evaluation measure?* Thousand Oaks, Calif.: Corwin Press.

Schalock, H.D., and M.D. Schalock. 1993. Student learning in teacher evaluation and school improvement: An introduction. *Journal of Personnel Evaluation in Education,* 7: 103-104.

Schalock, H.D., M. D. Schalock, and G. Girod. 1997. Teacher Work Sample Methodology as used at Western Oregon State University. In J. Millman (Ed.), *Grading teachers, grading schools: Is student achievement a valid evaluation measure?* Thousand Oaks, Calif.: Corwin Press.

Scriven, M. 1994. Duties of the teacher. *Journal of Personnel Evaluation in Education,* 8: 151-184.

Shufflebeam, D.L. 1997. Oregon Teacher Work Sample Methodology: Educational policy review. In J. Millman (Ed.) *Grading teachers, grading schools: Is student achievement a valid evaluation measure?* Thousand Oaks, Calif.: Corwin Press.

Stronge, J.H. 1997. Improving schools through teacher evaluation. In J. H. Stronge (Ed.) *Evaluating teaching: A guide to current thinking and best practice.* Thousand Oaks, Calif.: Corwin Press.

Sykes, G. 1997. On trial: The Dallas value-added accountability system. In J. Millman (Ed.), *Grading teachers, grading shools: Is student achievement a valid evaluation measure?* Thousand Oaks, Calif.: Corwin Press.

Thompson School District. August 1996. *A parent's guide to standards.* Loveland, Colo.: Author.

———. 1997-98. Teacher Professional Standards. *Thompson School District R2-J School Professional Evaluation Handbook.* Loveland, Colo.: Author: 4-5.

———. ND. School professional evaluation: Toolkit for administrators and school professionals. Loveland, Colo.: Author.

Thum, Y.M., and A.S. Bryk. 1997. Value-added productivity indicators: The Dallas system. In J. Millman (Ed.), *Grading teachers, grading schools: Is student achievement a valid evaluation measure?* Thousand Oak, Calif.: Corwin Press.

Traina, R.P. January 20, 1999. What makes a good teacher? *Education Week,* 18: 34.

University of Tennessee Value-Added Research and Assessment Center. 1997. *Graphical summary of educational findings from the Tennessee Value-Added Assessment System.* Knoxville, Tenn.: Author.

Viader. D., and J. Blair. September 29, 1999. Error affects test results in six states. *Education Week,* XIX(5):1, 13-15.

Walberg, H.J., and S.J. Paik. 1997. Assessment requires incentives to add value: A review of the Tennessee value-added assessment system. In J. Millman (Ed.), *Grading teachers, grading schools: Is student achievement a valid evaluation measure?* Thousand Oaks, Calif.: Corwin Press.

Webster, W.J., and R.L. Mendro. 1997. The Dallas value-added accountability system. In J. Millman (Ed.), *Grading teachers, grading schools: Is student achievement a valid evaluation measure?* Thousand Oaks, Calif.: Corwin Press.

Webster, W.J., R.L. Mendro, T. Orsak. D. Weerasinghe, and K. Bembry. 1997. Little practical difference and pie in the sky: A response to Thum and Bryk and a rejoinder to Sykes. In J. Millman (Ed.) *Grading teachers, grading schools: Is student achievement a valid evaluation measure?* Thousand Oaks, Calif.: Corwin Press.

Western Oregon University. ND. *Teacher Effectiveness Project—The reliability and validity of Teacher Work Sample Methodology: A synopsis.* Monmouth, Ore.: Author.

Wheeler, P.H. 1995. Before you use student tests in teacher evaluation…consider these issues. *AASPA Report.* Virginia Beach, Va.: American Association of School Personnel Administrators.

Wolfe, K., G. Lichtenstein, and C. Stevenson. 1997. Portfolios in teacher evaluation. In J.H. Stronge (Ed.) *Evaluating teaching: A guide to current thinking and best practice.* Thousand Oaks, Calif.: Corwin Press.

Wright, S.P., S. P. Horn, and W. L. Sanders, 1997. Teacher and classroom context effects on student achievement: Implications for teacher evaluation. *Journal of Personnel Evaluation in Education,* 11: 57-67.